15-77

How to install a

FIREPLACE

radiant heat▪circulating hot air free standing ▪ masonry

Donald R. Brann

Library of Congress Card No. 67-15264

THIRD PRINTING — 1976
REVISED EDITION

Published by
DIRECTIONS SIMPLIFIED, INC.

Division of
**EASI-BILD PATTERN CO., INC.
Briarcliff Manor, NY 10510**

FIRST PRINTING
© 1974

REVISED EDITION
1976

ISBN 0-87733-674-1

"ONCE UPON A TIME"

Those old enough to have been born during the time when all children's stories began with the magic words, "Once Upon A Time", can recall many favorites that fired their imagination. As children we were encouraged to believe everything was possible, and if anyone could learn to do something, so could we. All we had to do was play in the fresh air, breathe deeply, eat our spinach, and try, try, try. The word try, we were told, had magic. It meant The Real You.

In those days time was measured in years. Our parents took time to live, to cultivate friendship, to build a home and a marriage. Today we live a far different life, one dictated by split second decisions. Unless we swerve right instead of left, go around a darkened area instead of through, we gamble on survival.

With instant coffee, instant oatmeal, and other easy to prepare foods, every little girl grows up to become an instant cook. And thanks to prepared mortar mixes, prefabricated fireplace units, and simplified directions, every boy who dreamed of becoming a builder, can make like a pro installing a fireplace. The magic we believed as children is now packaged and sold in many lumber yards and home improvement centers, and many are still available in economy size packages.

Building a fireplace no longer requires special skills or months of planning. Read through this book, then select the components required. Since a fireplace increases the value and sales appeal of your home while it provides additional warmth to the way you live, it's an investment that creates an instant and important Capital Gains.

Don R. Brann

TABLE OF CONTENTS

HOT AIR CIRCULATING

SELECT TYPE
OF FIREPLACE

FREE STANDING

MASONRY

READ, LEARN, THEN BUY

To install a fireplace like a pro, learn what goes where and when. Read through this book. Evaluate the many options. The author has repeated many steps of installation to place same in context with each type of fireplace.

Lending institutions readily admit a fireplace adds considerable value to a house, while most owners agree it adds much to their home life. A fireplace is no ordinary improvement. To most people it's a dream come true. They believe a fireplace and a home are synonymous — you can't have one without the other.

The Underwriters Listed metal fireplace units and prefabricated chimney sections illustrated, permit making an installation that meets most building codes. When installed exactly as manufacturer specifies, the fireplace is approved for zero clearance to any combustible surface. This permits placing the unit on a finished floor and framing in with 2 x 4's as step-by-step directions suggest. The insulated housing and prefabricated hearth meet or surpass insurance company requirements.

If local building codes require a permit, ask your retailer for the Underwriters' Laboratories, Inc., and International Conference of Building Officials' code numbers that have been approved for the unit selected.

Since every fireplace installation contains a combination of elements that require some, or all of the components described, it's essential to read every page and note each illustration. Directions cover installation of a single fireplace as well as multiple units. Successfully installing one provides experience needed to do others. Those interested in a full or part time business opportunity will find fireplace installation a lucrative field.

To estimate what components are required, refer to Illus. 1. Measure distance A, B, C and D. The prefabricated chimney should terminate a minimum of 3'0" above roof, or 2' above highest point of roof within ten feet, or amount local codes specify. It should project 3' above a flat roof Illus.182.

Installing a fireplace requires no special tools other than a heavy duty saber saw, plus tin or aviation snips, Illus. 146. It does require following direction and making one promise.

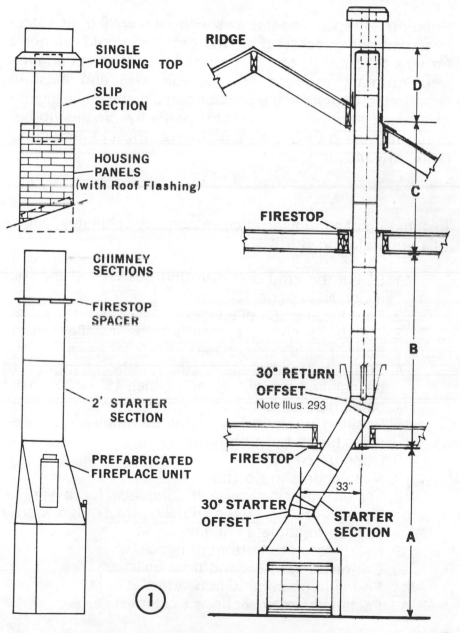

SINGLE HOUSING TOP

SLIP SECTION

HOUSING PANELS (with Roof Flashing)

CHIMNEY SECTIONS

FIRESTOP SPACER

2' STARTER SECTION

PREFABRICATED FIREPLACE UNIT

RIDGE

D

C

FIRESTOP

B

30° RETURN OFFSET
Note Illus. 293

FIRESTOP

33"

30° STARTER OFFSET

STARTER SECTION

A

①

Only work when you feel physically fit, and only for as long as you think clearly. Don't rush. Don't work when you get tired or after an argument. It's at this time errors and accidents occur. Remember, a fireplace is a lifetime investment, one that will bring you and your family many, many hours of peace, relaxation and togetherness.

Building a fireplace so it draws without smoking, produces heat without generating a draught that could trigger a furnace thermostat; one that burns wood at an economical rate, normally requires considerable skill and masonry experience. Thanks to the prefabricated metal units, anyone can install a fireplace that draws perfectly, creates no bad draughts, and provides an abundance of warm air without doing any masonry work.

Installation of a fireplace and prefabricated chimney follows this general procedure*:

1. Select the kind and size unit best suited for your room. Note page 12.
2. Zero in on exact placement.
3. Decide whether fireplace is to be installed on the floor or on a raised base.
4. Survey room above to decide whether chimney is to be installed straight up, or inclined 15° or 30° to the back, right or left.
5. Position fireplace. Frame in shoe, studs and plate on sides but not in front of unit.
6. Open up ceiling.
7. Nail headers in position.
8. Fasten starter section to fireplace for a vertical installation; or fasten starter offset, then starter section to angle a chimney.
9. Nail firestop to bottom of headers.
10. Cut opening in second floor ceiling.
11. Frame in opening with headers.
12. Fasten chimney sections to starter.

10

13. Nail firestop to top of header in floor of attic.
14. Frame opening in roof.
15. Continue chimney installation so it, and/or slip section, allows flue to finish 3' above roof line.
16. Cut chimney housing to pitch of roof. Bend high side of housing.
17. Fasten housing to flashing.
18. Remove raincap.
19. Position housing and flashing over opening.
20. Insert slip section.
21. Raise shingles. Apply asphalt cement. Nail flashing to roof.
22. Replace raincap or wind cap.
23. Install ducts and fan for forced hot air circulating fireplace.
24. Finish framing on face of fireplace.
25. Apply gypsum wallboard or hardwood paneling to framing.
26. Apply slate, tile, marble, brick facing or any other noncombustible material around opening.*
27. Install hearth.
28. Install grilles over ducts.
29. Build a mantel.

All components illustrated in this book were designed to simplify installation. All parts fit together without special tools or experience. If any section of chimney, offset, starter section or elbow doesn't fit perfectly, don't force it. Tell your dealer. He will either replace a faulty unit or explain where you went wrong.

Since a fireplace requires buying items few people have previously purchased, the author suggests shopping around to find those illustrated or their equivalent. Buy all accessories from one source. Don't improvise. The manufacturer of the components illustrated employs skilled fireplace experts as field representatives. While they don't make any installations, you or your fireplace dealer can get all the free advice needed to solve any special situation.

*Always read and follow manufacturer's directions.

CHOOSING A LOCATION

To envision how a fireplace will affect placement of furniture and/or traffic through a room, make a full size paper, hardboard or corrugated board pattern to overall size of the unit, including the hearth, Illus. 2. Your home improvement retailer can provide overall dimensions for the unit you select. Overall sizes of various models are shown on page 237. Make a second template to indicate space chimney requires, i.e., 18 x 18", 18 x 21" or 18 x 26", Illus. 3.

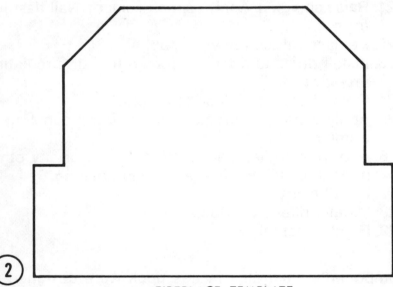

FIREPLACE TEMPLATE

One way to zero in on size of opening is to add the width to length of the room, use the total as a guide. For example: a room measuring 16 x 20 = 36. This indicates a fireplace with a 36" opening, Illus. 6, 10.

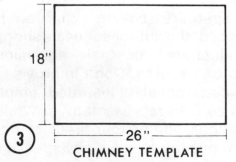

18"

26"

CHIMNEY TEMPLATE

Position the fireplace template where it complements furnishings without creating a traffic problem, and where it simplifies installing a chimney. Depending on size of fireplace, you won't want any furniture less than 5' from opening. A hot fire can keep you and your furniture a good six feet away.

Using the full size template, rather than snapping chalk lines on the floor, emphasizes size. The fireplaces described in this book can be installed in any position indicated, Illus. 4.

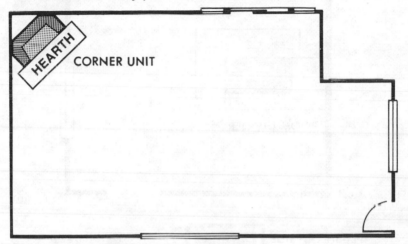

CORNER UNIT

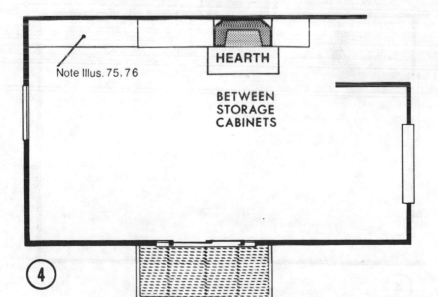

Note Illus. 75, 76

HEARTH

BETWEEN
STORAGE
CABINETS

4

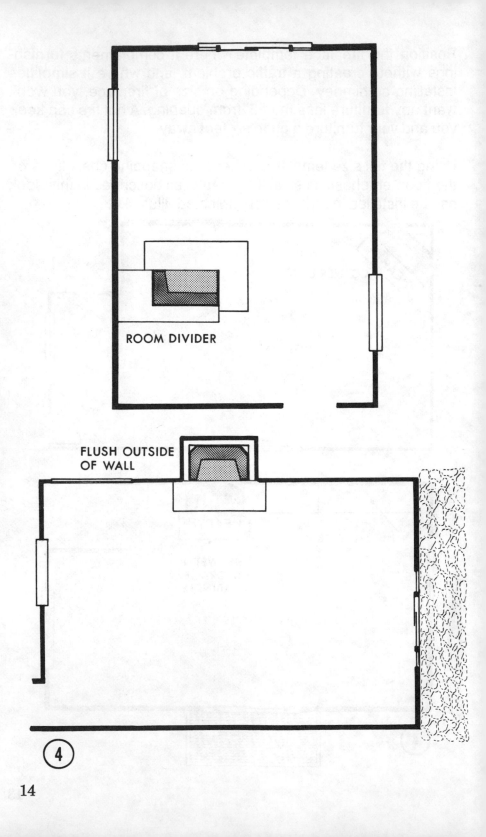

ROOM DIVIDER

FLUSH OUTSIDE
OF WALL

4

14

To locate position for a chimney, it's first necessary to zero in on location for fireplace. After template indicates an acceptable location, decide whether the chimney can be installed straight up, angle 15° or 30° to the back, right or left.

This book simplifies installation of a free standing unit, Illus. 5, that's perfect for a cabin, add-a-room, or when transforming a garage into living space; to radiant heat and hot air circulating units. Decorative gas and electric fireplaces can be installed by following directions starting on page 173.

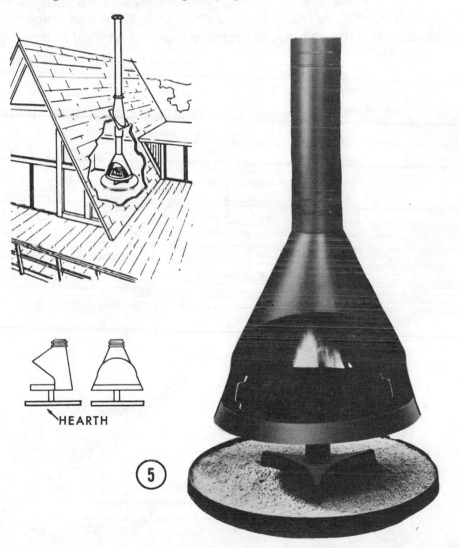

HEARTH

⑤

RADIANT HEAT FIREPLACE

The radiant heat fireplace, Illus. 6, is designed to produce as much, or more heat, than one constructed with firebrick. This unit comes complete with a raised refractory hearth that draws cold air at floor level. The unit can be placed on a finished floor, Illus. 7, or on a raised base, Illus. 8. The base can be 2 x 4 on edge (3½"); 2 x 6 (5½"), 2 x 8, or on a raised platform, page 126. The entire unit can be installed in any position shown, Illus. 4. Installation follows same step-by-step procedure described for a hot air circulating unit with one important exception. This unit doesn't require the cold air inlet and hot air outlet ducts.

Whether framed in with 2 x 4 or enclosed within a masonry chimney, this unit produces an enormous amount of radiant heat.

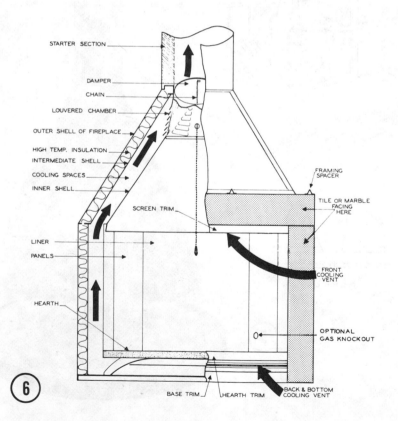

STARTER SECTION

DAMPER

CHAIN

LOUVERED CHAMBER

OUTER SHELL OF FIREPLACE

HIGH TEMP. INSULATION
INTERMEDIATE SHELL
COOLING SPACES
INNER SHELL

FRAMING SPACER

SCREEN TRIM

TILE OR MARBLE FACING HERE

LINER
PANELS

FRONT COOLING VENT

HEARTH

OPTIONAL GAS KNOCKOUT

6

BASE TRIM   HEARTH TRIM

BACK & BOTTOM COOLING VENT

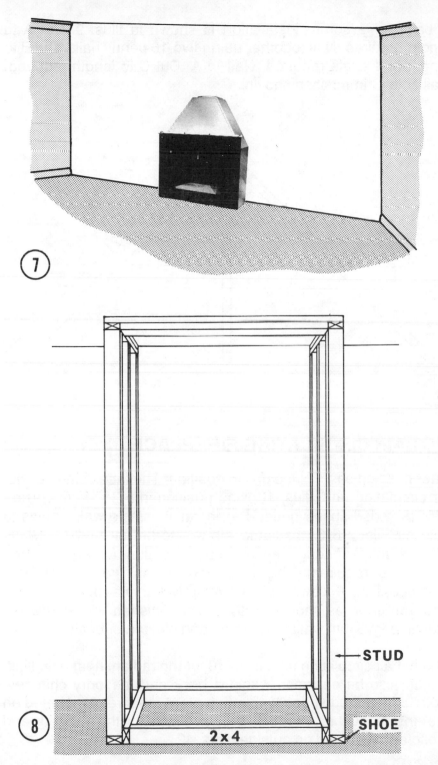

⑦

⑧   2 x 4

STUD

SHOE

17

A base for a corner installation is shown in Illus. 9. Cut A to length required. Nail together using two 16 penny nails. Cut B to length and angle required. Nail to A. Cut C to length required. Nail B to C in position shown.

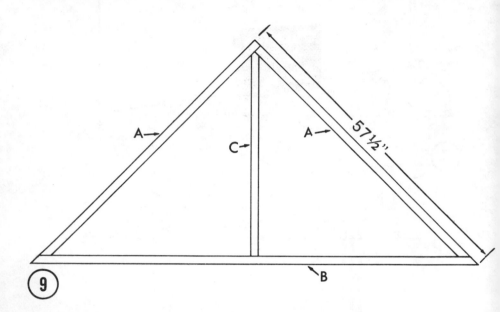

9

HOT AIR CIRCULATING FIREPLACE

After building base, place unit in position. The face of the 36" hot air circulating unit, Illus. 10, was positioned 57½" from corner. This provided space needed to install 6" single wall elbows to cold air inlets; 6½" insulated elbows to hot air outlet. Always move a unit far enough out from corner to allow for elbows when same are required. This unit, as well as the radiant heat fireplace, Illus. 6, can be placed entirely within a room, Illus. 11, and framed in as shown. Both can be finished with hardwood paneling, gypsum wallboard, lathe and plaster, or brick.

The hot air circulating unit, Illus. 10, or the radiant heat unit, Illus. 6, can also be enclosed within a brick and masonry chimney. Both units are equipped with a two piece firescreen mounted on the inside. Other models are available with a hood and firescreen mounted on outside, Illus. 42.

18

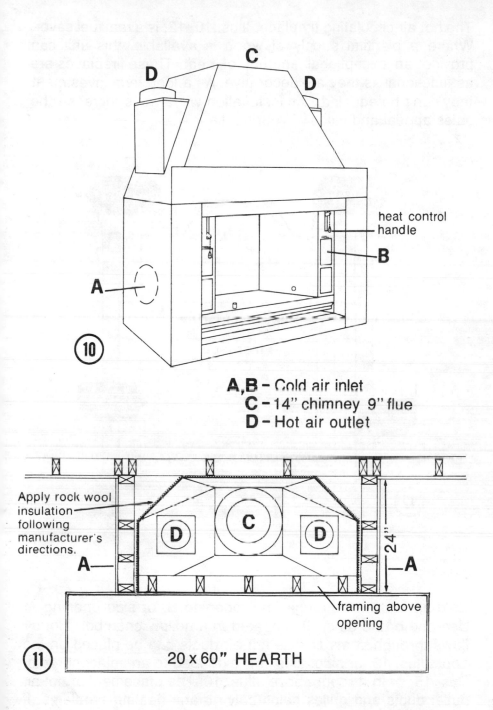

heat control handle

B

A

⑩

A,B – Cold air inlet
C – 14" chimney 9" flue
D – Hot air outlet

Apply rock wool insulation following manufacturer's directions.

A

24"

A

framing above opening

⑪   20 x 60" HEARTH

The hot air circulating fireplace, Illus. 10, 12, is a real fuel saver. Where a plentiful supply of wood is available, this unit can provide an exceptional amount of heat. These fireplaces are as functional as they are decorative. As a long term investment they can't be equaled. An installation will always increase the sales appeal and value of your house.

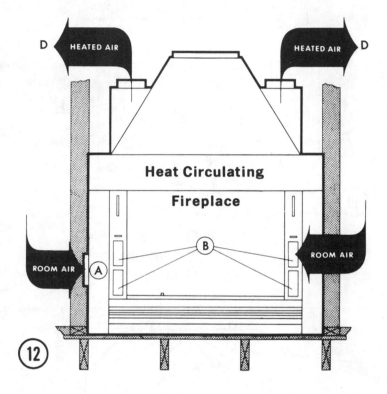

Cold air is drawn through front opening B, or side opening A. Use one or the other. It is heated in a hollow chamber. Hot air flows through vents D. The hot air ducts can be placed on the front, Illus. 13, or side, Illus. 14; extended to an adjacent room, Illus. 15; or in a room above, Illus. 16. The placement of hot air outlet ducts and grilles helps solve many heating problems. If the unit projects completely into a room, hot air ducts can be positioned on the side, Illus. 17.

Two each of the numbered duct parts are included with fireplace.
① 6" duct
② 12" duct
③ 90° adjustable elbow
④ hot air outlet assembly

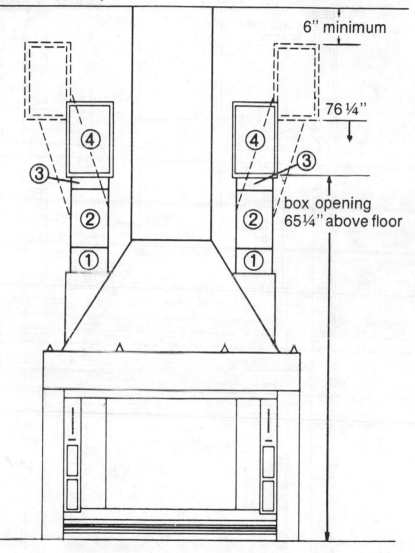

6" minimum

76 ¼"

box opening
65¼" above floor

⑬

21

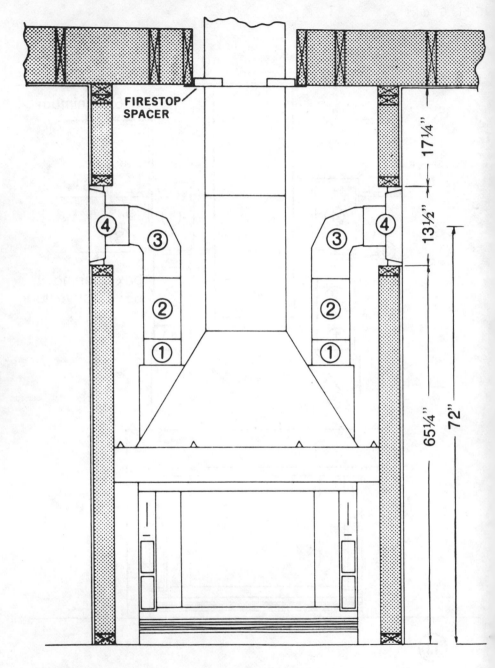

FIRESTOP
SPACER

17¼"

13½"

65¼"

72"

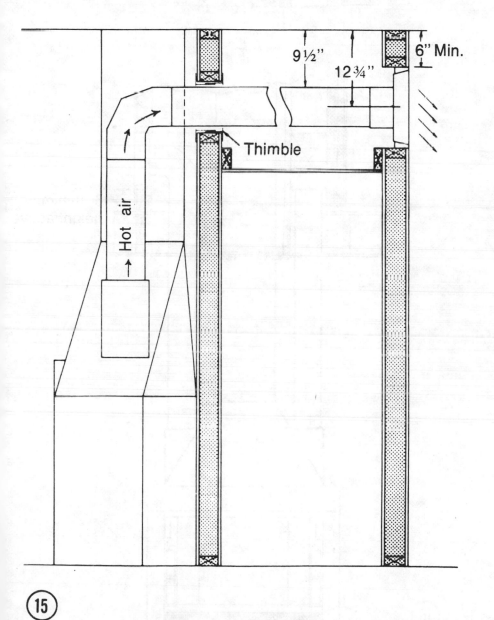

9½"

12¾"

6" Min.

Thimble

Hot air

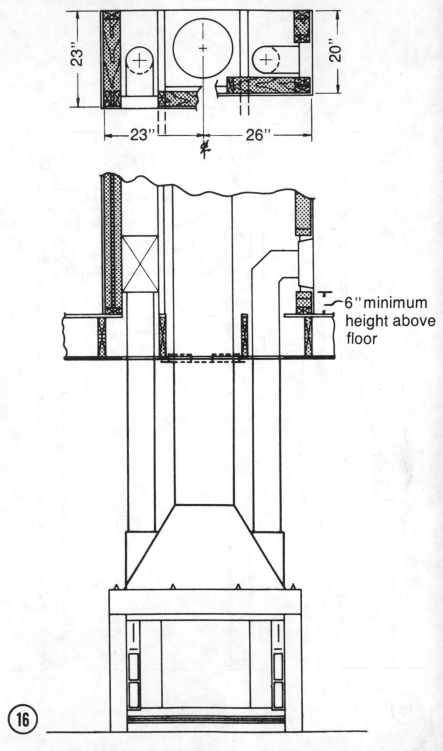

6" minimum height above floor

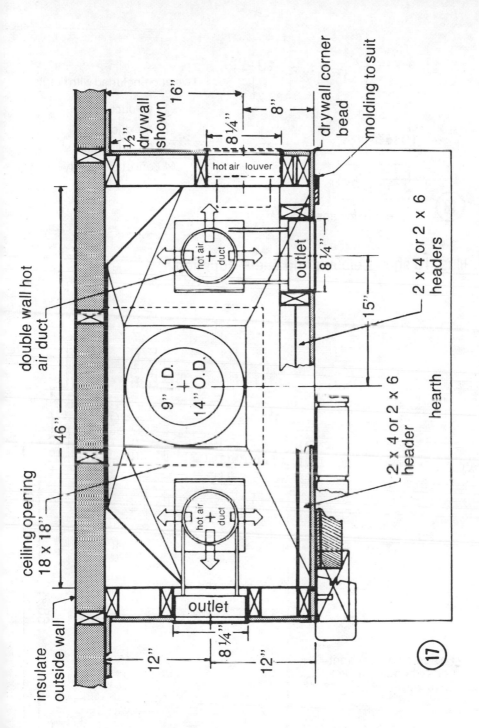

insulate outside wall

ceiling opening 18 x 18"

double wall hot air duct

46"

12"

8 ¼"

12"

outlet

hot air duct

9" I.D. 14" O.D.

hot air duct

2 x 4 or 2 x 6 header

2 x 4 or 2 x 6 headers

15"

8 ¼"

outlet

hot air louver

8 ¼"

drywall shown

½"

16"

8"

drywall corner bead

molding to suit

hearth

⑰

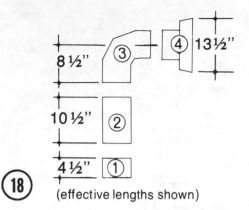

Two each included with fireplace.

① 6" duct
② 12" duct
③ 90° adjustable elbow
④ outlet assembly

(18)

(effective lengths shown)

Illus. 18 shows elbows and ducts supplied.

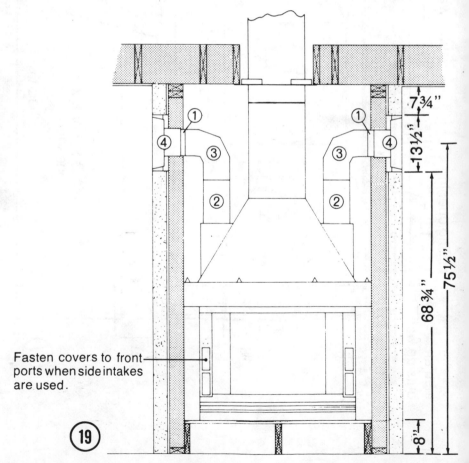

Fasten covers to front ports when side intakes are used.

(19)

26

Illus. 19 shows hot air ducts connected to grille on the side of a raised unit projecting into a room.

Always install grilles with louvers down using screws provided, Illus. 20.

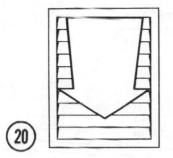

After installing hot and cold air ducts, complete framing in across front as shown, Illus. 21. The header rests on A spacers welded across front of fireplace. Toenail header to studs using 8 penny nails. Install a double 2 x 6 header in position shown if building inspector requires same,

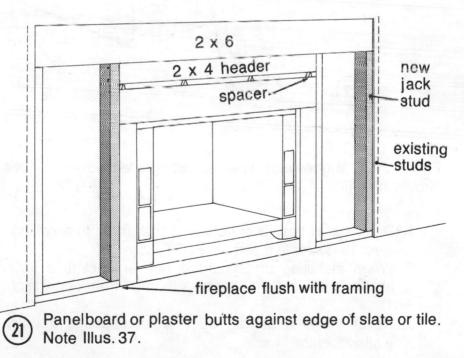

2 x 6

2 x 4 header

spacer

new jack stud

existing studs

fireplace flush with framing

Panelboard or plaster butts against edge of slate or tile. Note Illus. 37.

A room at some distance from fireplace can be heated if fans, Illus. 22, are installed in cold air ducts. The fans create a constant and even flow of warm air through duct work. Never install fans in warm air ducts. Wiring instructions for installing fans are shown in Illus. 307

Fan housing projects distance equal to thickness of wall material

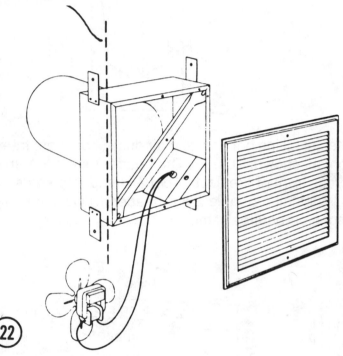

Follow these suggestions when selecting a location for a hot air circulating unit:

1. Don't install hot air outlets closer than 6" to a ceiling, Illus. 13, 15, or to a corner.
2. When installing an extended hot air duct to a floor above, don't install outlet less than 6" from floor, Illus. 16.
3. Never install a hot air duct to an opposite parallel wall within 24".

Remove 6" diameter discs on side. Remove and discard insulation behind disc. Make certain opening is completely clean. Bend tabs out, Illus. 23. Use 6" diameter, locally purchased, galvanized pipe or elbows to draw cold air through a side, port A, Illus. 10, or from an adjacent room. Always install crimped end of 6" pipe into side of fireplace. Fasten pipe to housing with sheet metal screws through tabs, Illus. 23.

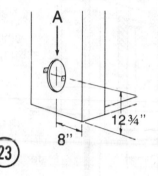

When cold air ducts are connected to opening on side, covers, Illus. 24, are screwed in position to close front cold air inlets. These covers must be used when fans are installed in cold air inlets.

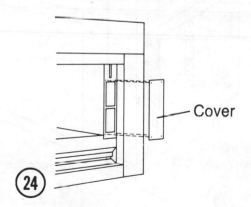

Cover

2 x 4 end wall framing, Illus. 25, provides opening for fan. Project fan housing, Illus. 26, distance equal to thickness of wall material. If you cover a wall frame with ¼" plywood, project edge of fan housing ¼". Note page 208 for fan installation. Always frame openings to exact size manufacturer specifies.

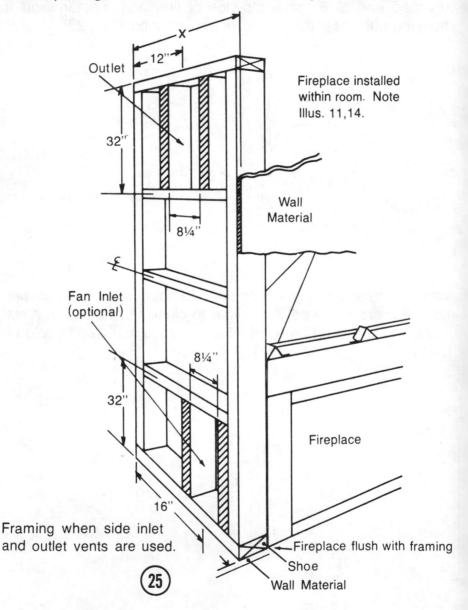

Fireplace installed within room. Note Illus. 11,14.

Outlet

x

12"

32"

8¼"

Wall Material

Fan Inlet (optional)

8¼"

32"

Fireplace

16"

Framing when side inlet and outlet vents are used.

Fireplace flush with framing

Shoe

Wall Material

25

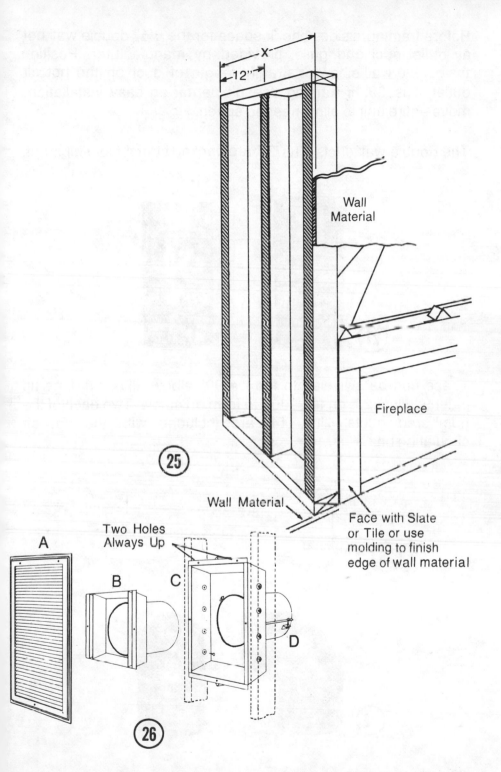

X

12"

Wall
Material

Fireplace

Wall Material

Face with Slate
or Tile or use
molding to finish
edge of wall material

㉕

Two Holes
Always Up

A

B

C

D

㉖

31

Before framing in sides check space for the 6½" double wall hot air outlet duct and grille, provided by manufacturer. Position the double wall elbow or straight length of duct on the hot air outlet, Illus. 32. If framing doesn't permit an easy installation, move entire unit to allow needed space.

The double wall ducts, Illus. 27, are packed straight for shipment.

These can be swiveled to form a 90° elbow, Illus. 28. Line up indents, Illus. 29, on top edge to form an elbow. Two each of the numbered ducts, Illus. 14, are included with the hot air circulating unit, Illus. 10.

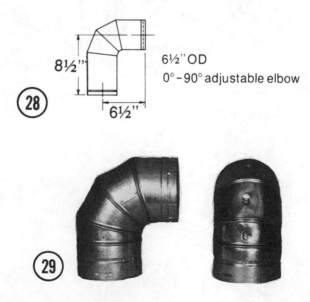

6½"OD
0°–90° adjustable elbow

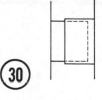

wall thimble
adjusts for 3½" to 6" walls
Note Illus. 15

(30)

An adjustable wall thimble, Illus. 30, is also available from your retailer. This adjusts from 3½ to 6". The manufacturer also provides telescoping duct in various sizes from 4½, 6½, 12 to 18", Illus. 31.

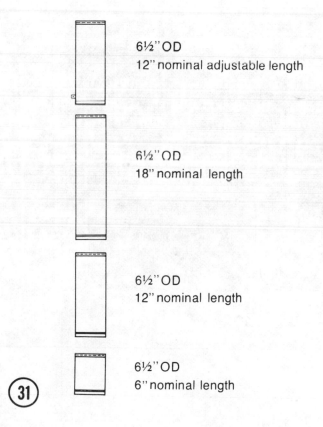

6½" OD
12" nominal adjustable length

6½" OD
18" nominal length

6½" OD
12" nominal length

6½" OD
6" nominal length

(31)

The hot air cover on opening, Illus. 32, should not be removed until you are ready to attach a hot air elbow or straight duct. At that time, untwist and remove wire, cover, insulation and thin metal washer.

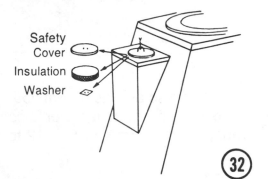

Safety
Cover

Insulation

Washer

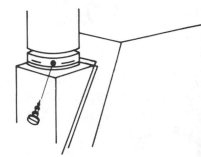

(32)

(32)

Safety covers provide insurance you won't use a fireplace until the hot air ducts are connected. The Heat Control Handles at left and right of firescreen, Illus. 10, cannot function until safely covers are removed. The safety covers also keep debris out of chamber. After removing wire and after connecting hot air ducts, check heat control handles to make certain they work perfectly. Read and follow all directions manufacturer packs with each piece of equipment. After completing installation of hot and cold air ducts, complete framing in front of unit, Illus. 33. While a 2 x 4 header resting on A spacers is ample, if a building inspector suggests using 2 x 6, install same.

1953256

(33)

Everyone who is physically able, can easily do all the work with one exception. Because of a heart, eye or ear condition, some people should not work on a roof. In this case farm this part of the job out to a roofer. Those willing to work on the roof will find a body harness, Illus. 159, and roofers' safety line, Illus. 160, as described on page 109 a big help.

A fireplace with a 28" screened opening requires a prefabricated chimney with a 7" ID (inside dimension) flue; the 36" and larger openings, Illus. 34, require a 9" ID flue. Both units can be installed in any position shown, Illus. 4. Both can be faced with brick, Illus. 35; tile, Illus. 36; slate, Illus. 37; black glass, or left flat black or painted, Illus. 38.

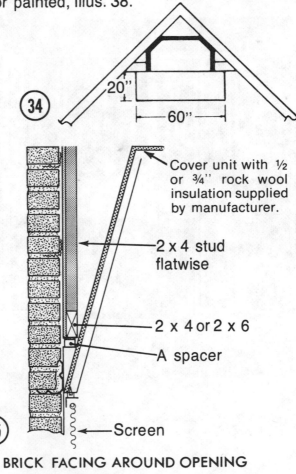

BRICK FACING AROUND OPENING
AND OR FIREPLACE WALL

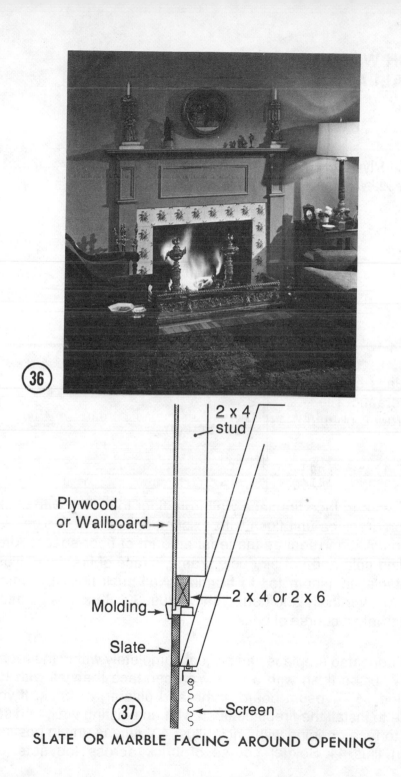

36

Plywood
or Wallboard →

2 x 4
stud

Molding →

2 x 4 or 2 x 6

Slate →

37

← Screen

SLATE OR MARBLE FACING AROUND OPENING

FLUSH WALL INSTALLATION

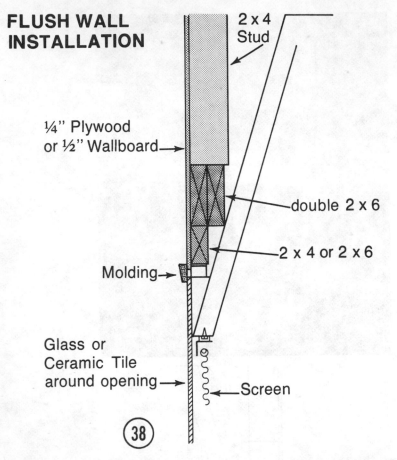

2 x 4 Stud

¼" Plywood or ½" Wallboard →

double 2 x 6

2 x 4 or 2 x 6

Molding →

Glass or Ceramic Tile around opening →

Screen ←

(38)

If you want to face fireplace wall from floor to ceiling with brick, position fireplace unit flush with existing finished wall, Illus. 35. This installation requires the least amount of floor space. After installing cold and hot air ducts, frame in face of fireplace, Illus. 33. Staple aluminum foil to framing. Nail brick ties to framing every 16" vertically and horizontally, Illus. 39. Bend ties so each projects into a course of brick.

A prefabricated fireplace can project completely within the room, Illus. 7, or be flush with a wall. You can face the wall with ¼" plywood, ½" gypsum board, lathe and plaster, or brick. If you decide to install the fireplace flush with an existing wall, and still want to face opening with brick, Illus. 40, recess unit in position shown, Illus. 41. Soldier course of brick across top sets on lintel.

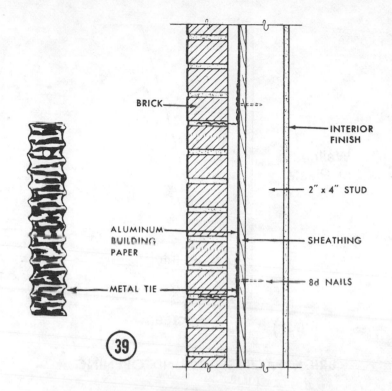

BRICK

INTERIOR FINISH

2" x 4" STUD

ALUMINUM BUILDING PAPER

SHEATHING

METAL TIE

8d NAILS

(39)

(40)

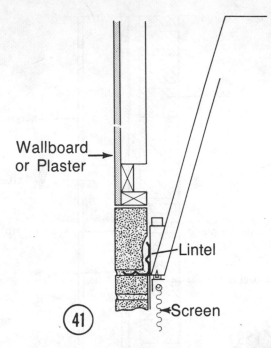

Wallboard or Plaster

Lintel

Screen

41

BRICK FACING AROUND OPENING

If you install a fireplace with a hood, Illus. 42, note position of lintel across top of hood. This provides support for a header course of brick, Illus. 43. In this installation, brick frames both sides and across top of opening.

An angle iron (lintel), Illus. 44, is embedded in mortar on course of brick equal to top of opening. This simplifies installation of brick across top of opening. Brick ties, Illus. 39, are nailed in position and bent out. These are embedded in every fourth to sixth course.

An important feature of a hot air circulating fireplace is that cold air can be ducted from two adjoining rooms just as hot air ducts can pipe warm air to adjacent rooms. Or both cold and hot air grilles can be placed on face of fireplace wall, Illus. 13.

By recessing the fireplace exact amount the brick, slate or tile facing requires, facing material can finish flush with existing plaster, wallboard or paneling.

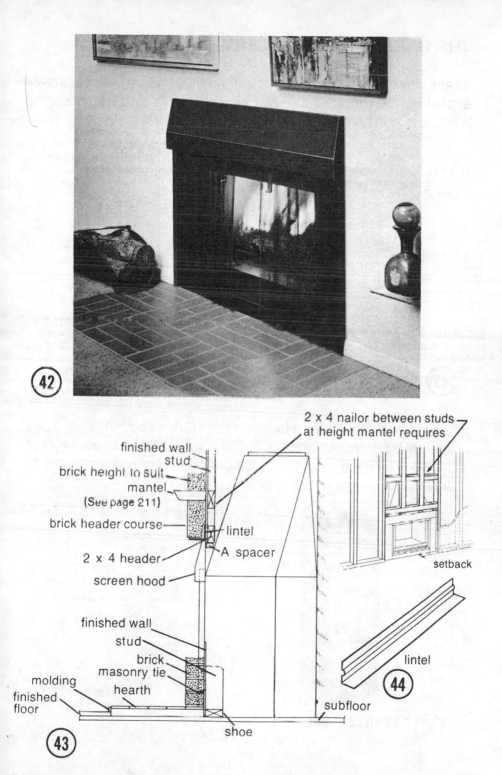

42

finished wall
stud
brick height to suit
mantel
(See page 211)

brick header course

2 x 4 header
screen hood

lintel
A spacer

2 x 4 nailor between studs
at height mantel requires

setback

finished wall
stud
brick
masonry tie

molding
finished
floor
hearth

subfloor

lintel

44

shoe

43

THE PREFABRICATED CHIMNEY

Thanks to the prefabricated chimney, Illus. 45, and accessories available, the radiant heat, hot air circulating and free standing fireplaces can be installed on top of a finished floor.

MINERAL INSULATION holds heat inside for maximum draft action without condensation.

STAINLESS STEEL INNER PIPE for long trouble-free life and added safety.

GALVANIZED STEEL OUTER PIPE gives added protection against weather and damage.

TWIST-LOCK CONNECTOR assures quick, permanent installation without additional bands or accessories

(45)

For a vertical chimney installation the starter section, Illus. 1, 46, provided by manufacturer, is fastened directly to fireplace, Illus. 47. Use 1" No. 8 sheet metal screws or screws provided by manufacturer.

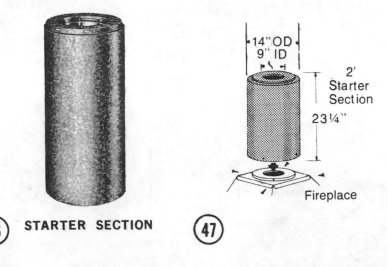

14" OD
9" ID

2'
Starter
Section

23¼"

Fireplace

(46) **STARTER SECTION**   (47)

To corbel a chimney 15° either to the back, right, or left, a 15° starter offset, Illus. 48, is fastened to bottom of the starter section. The assembled unit is then fastened to the fireplace. A 6", 2 or 3' chimney section can then be added, or the return offset can be twist locked directly to the starter section. All offsets and returns should be fastened with sheet metal screws.

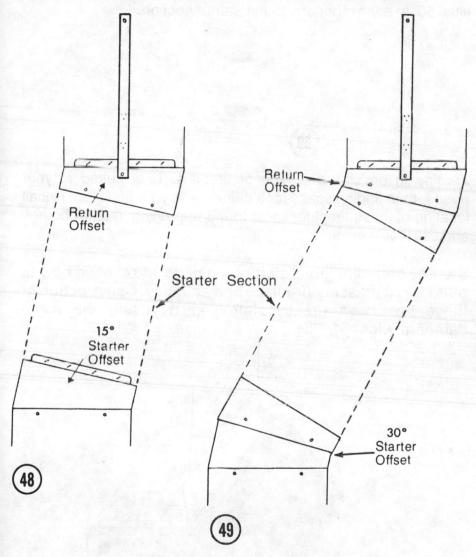

For a 30° offset, Illus. 49, the 30° starter offset is fastened to bottom of the starter section.

Since a chimney can be installed straight up, Illus. 1, or corbeled (angled) 15°, Illus. 48; or 30°, Illus. 49, to the back, right or left, it allows considerable choice in selecting a location for both the fireplace and the chimney.

The chimney comes in 6", 2' and 3' sections. Each twist locks, Illus. 50, to each other and to the starter section.

Zeroing in on size and type of fireplace best suited to your needs, then finding space for a chimney, is your first step. Recall location of those fireplaces you found appealing in other homes and use it as a guide.

Step-by-step directions starting on page 133 explain how to build an all masonry fireplace and chimney. Construction of these has been greatly simplified by using the metal dampers, Illus. 51, 234.

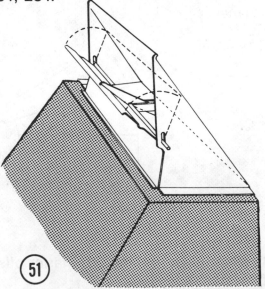

A brick faced fireplace connected to a prefabricated chimney requires no masonry foundation. The unit can be placed on a solid wood floor; or on a raised base; or on a platform, Illus. 52, 53. You can use 2 x 4, 2 x 6 or 2 x 8 on edge, Illus. 54, to build a raised base. Cut A to length required, cut B to overall depth. Nail B to A with two 16 penny nails if 2 x 4's are used; 3 nails if 2 x 6's are used. Place frame in position. Check with level. Use pieces of wood shingle to shim level. Toenail frame to floor after selecting exact location.

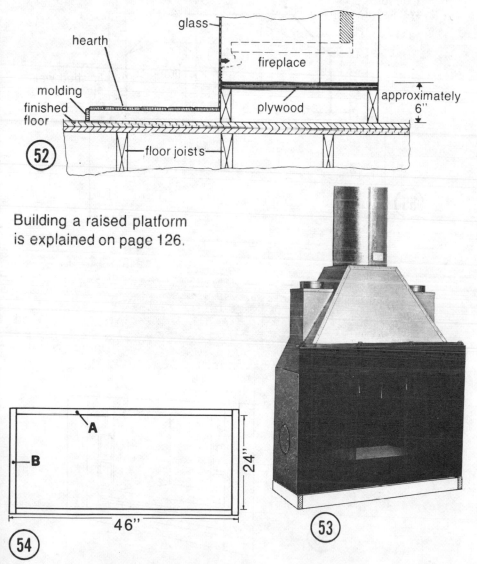

Building a raised platform is explained on page 126.

45

These prefabricated units can be installed completely within a room, Illus. 7, or flush with a wall, Illus. 55. If the location selected is in an outside wall, or in an unheated garage or breezeway, the unit must be insulated. Place unit on a pad of insulation. Apply 2" rock wool blanket to surface shown, Illus. 56. If you project the back of the unit into an adjoining room, build a wall-to-wall closet, Illus. 77, alongside.

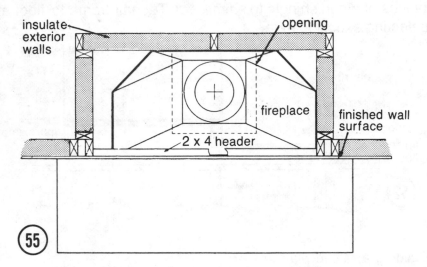

insulate exterior walls

opening

fireplace

finished wall surface

2 x 4 header

(55)

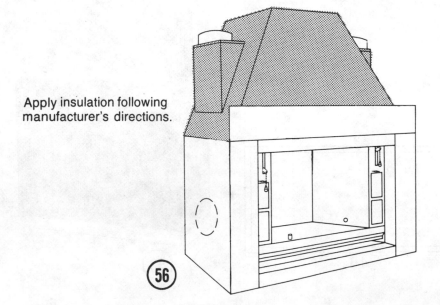

Apply insulation following manufacturer's directions.

(56)

When you want face of unit to finish flush with an existing wall, position unit as shown, Illus. 21, 57, 288.

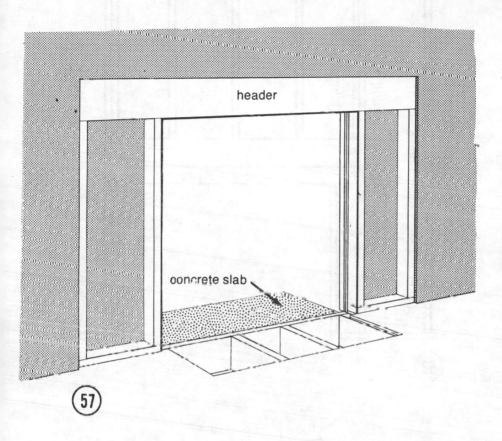

Always butt end framing against unit. If you place fireplace on a raised base, end framing butts against base. The two end frames hold unit in position while the offset and/or starter section and chimney is installed.

When unit is to be installed on the floor and flush with wall; or recessed amount required for tile, slate or brick facing, Illus. 35, knock out studs within area selected, Illus. 58. Cut off shoe. Build raised base if you want one. Position unit in place. Anchor unit with 1 x 2 blocks, Illus. 59. Reframe front with a header and studs after installing cold and hot air ducts, Illus. 33.

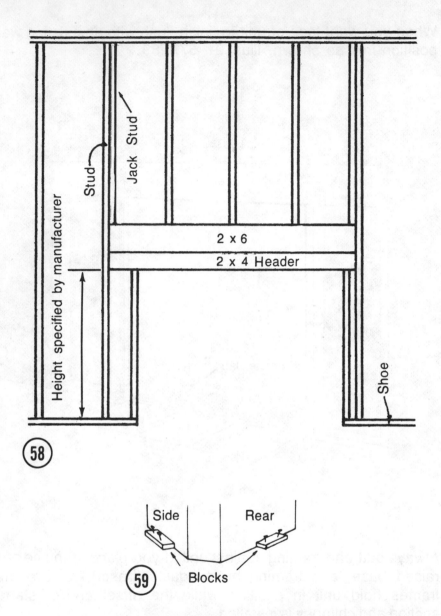

Height specified by manufacturer

Stud

Jack Stud

2 x 6

2 x 4 Header

Shoe

58

Side

Rear

59

Blocks

When making a flush wall installation in an outside wall, the unit should be placed on a wood, metal or concrete platform. If back of unit is outside of house and above grade, Illus. 60, you can build a supporting base in several different ways. You can dig down below frost level and pour a concrete base to height required; or you can nail outriggers to floor joists, Illus. 285, 288.

48

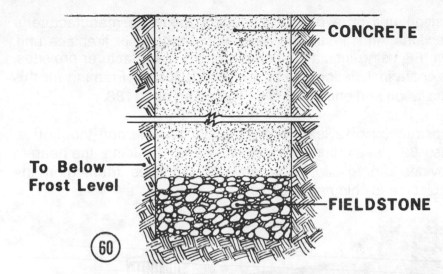

CONCRETE

To Below
Frost Level

FIELDSTONE

60

In new construction it's easier to spike outriggers to floor joists,
Insulate between outriggers, cover outriggers with two ¾"
plywood panels to equal height of finished floor. After installing
unit, enclose within 2 x 4 framing, Illus. 291. This should be
sided and painted to match exterior of house, Illus. 61.

61

Position unit on a pad of insulation following manufacturer's directions. After insulating back, sides and top of fireplace unit, Illus. 56, using insulation and directions manufacturer provides, the entire installation can be enclosed, Illus. 61. Framing for this installation and enclosure is explained on page 186.

Construction of a lean-to or free standing garden tool house, Illus. 62, is explained in Book #649. Building the lean-to provides storage for logs while it simplifies framing in the fireplace and chimney enclosure.

(62)

The Underwriters' Laboratories Listed units illustrated meet all fire and building code requirements when installed exactly as manufacturer specifies.

CORNER INSTALLATION

A popular installation is shown in Illus. 63. Here the fireplace is installed 45° across a corner. Follow manufacturer's directions and position template, or unit, where shown. Buy 6" single wall galvanized pipe elbows, Illus. 64, from any hardware, plumbing or heating supply house. Use these to connect the side cold air inlet to the grille manufacturer provides, or to fan, Illus. 26. Fasten tabs to elbow with ¾ or 1" sheet metal screws, or leave side vent intact, Illus. 10. Do not remove cover. Use cold air duct B on front.

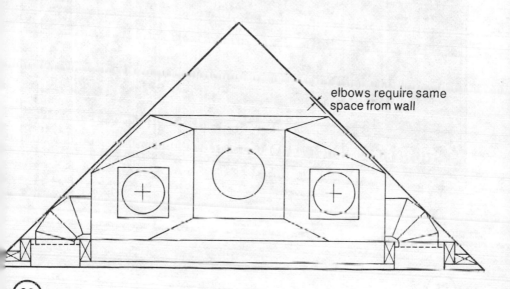

elbows require same space from wall

(63)

(64)

Prior to placing unit in a corner or against a wall, Illus. 17, ascertain whether adjacent walls are insulated. If framing is exposed, Illus. 65, staple insulation to studs within fireplace enclosure. Loose insulation can be blown in if you don't want to remove sound wall covering.

(65)

If you prefer to install a raised fireplace, one that will be faced with brick, keep in mind most face brick measures 2¼". Allow a ⅜" mortar joint. This establishes an increment of 2⅝". Four courses of brick equals 10½".

To simplify estimating where a cold air inlet will fit into a course of brick, and to make certain a course of brick is laid at exact height lintel requires for course across opening, Illus. 35, make a 1 x 2 story pole, Illus. 66. Draw lines at 2⅝, 5¼, 7⅞, 10½", etc., etc. Use this to lay out each course of brick. Some folding rules have brick courses printed on the back.

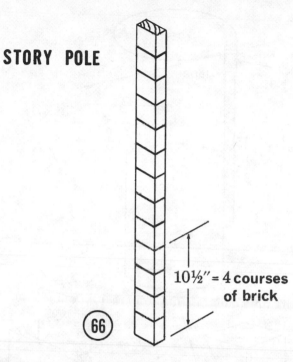

STORY POLE

10½" = 4 **courses of brick**

66

CHIMNEY THROUGH HOUSE

After positioning unit either on the floor or on a raised base, working from planks across two sawhorses, drop a plumb bob down from ceiling so point of bob touches each corner of unit. Mark ceiling to indicate each corner. Snap chalk lines on ceiling to indicate exact position for 2 x 4 plate.

If chimney is to be corbeled, place a starter offset, plus the chimney starter section in position, Illus. 49. If a vertical installation is being made, fasten chimney starter section to top of fireplace, Illus. 47.

Using a pencil fastened to end of a 1 x 3" x 3' straight edge,* Illus. 67, draw outline of chimney opening on ceiling. Draw circle on ceiling so it allows 2" clearance for chimney. You can now remove the offset and/or starter section. This provides more room to open up ceiling. After making a test opening to ascertain what's inside, use a saber saw, Illus. 68, or keyhole saw to cut opening.

*Cut to 2" width.

53

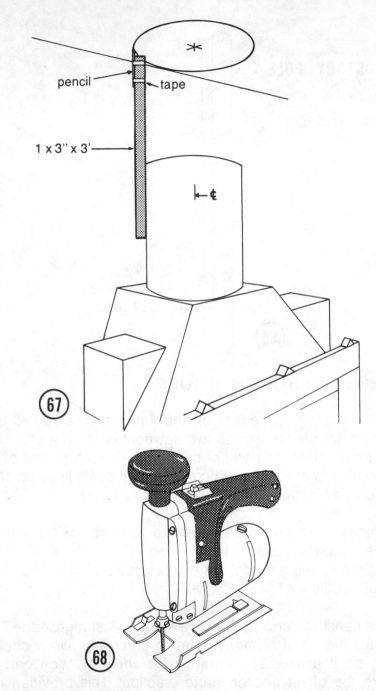

pencil — tape

1 x 3" x 3'

＊

¢

67

68

Use care when selecting a location for a chimney. Don't saw a hole in space containing water, waste or vent lines, electric cable, or a hot water line serving baseboard radiation.

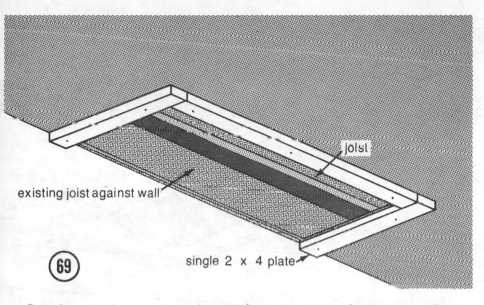

existing joist against wall

joist

single 2 x 4 plate

(69)

Cut 2 x 4 plate to length needed, Illus. 69. Spike plate flat to ceiling joists using 16 penny nails. Drive nails into joists. These are usually spaced 16" on centers. When a plate runs parallel to joists, and can't be nailed, drill ¼" holes through plate and ceiling and fasten plate in position with toggle bolts, Illus. 70. While a single 2 x 4 plate is usually O.K., some building inspectors may require your using a double 2 x 4 plate. Always overlap joints, Illus. 71, when installing a double plate.

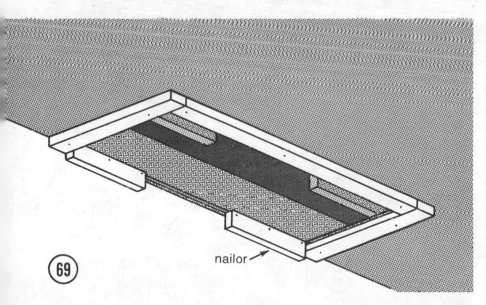

nailor

(69)

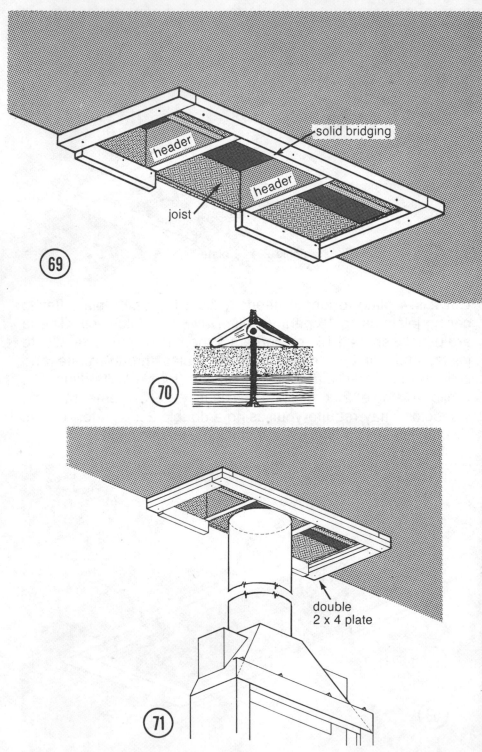

solid bridging

header

header

joist

69

70

double
2 x 4 plate

71

56

Using a plumb bob, check exact location for shoe, Illus. 25. The 2 x 4 shoe butts against fireplace or alongside a raised base. This secures unit in position. Spike shoe to floor with 16 penny nails.

Cut 2 x 4 studs to length required so each has to be driven in position and holds its position without nailing. Don't cut them so they force plate into ceiling. Toenail studs to shoe and plate 16" on center using 8 penny nails. When you install this framing, you don't have to use blocks, Illus. 59, to hold unit in place.

The 2 x 4 shoe, studs and plate for a fireplace installed within a room provide support when cutting joists for chimney opening. When a fireplace is installed on a first floor, the chimney will frequently go through a bedroom. The 9" flue for a vertical chimney installation requires an 18 x 18" opening. Cut opening to size specified when installing a chimney inclined 15° or 30°.

The prefabricated chimney can go through a closet, or a closet can be built around. Or a floor to ceiling cabinet, Illus. 72, can be built following directions on page 177.

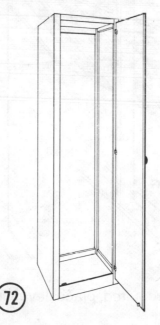

(72)

57

The insulated chimney produces a warm drying space. Hinge doors on this cabinet. Fasten a fold-down towel hanger on inside of door. When the fireplace is being used, dry out wet socks or other small articles.

When cutting an opening through roof, locate and mark opening on rafters. Nail a temporary 2 x 4 brace, Illus. 73, across rafters prior to cutting rafter or sawing sheathing. After nailing headers, Illus. 74, to rafters, the 2 x 4 bracing can be removed.

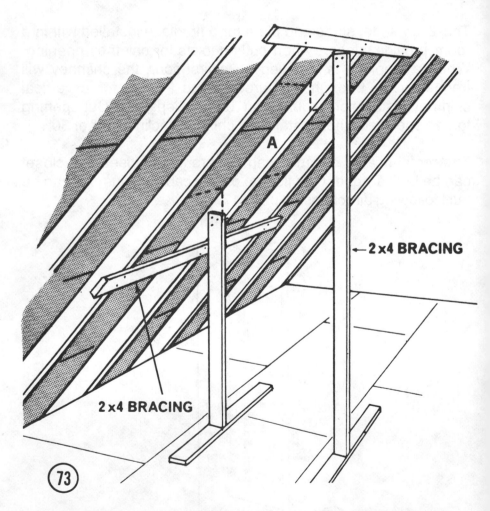

A

←2 x 4 BRACING

2 x 4 BRACING

(73)

To cut rafter to angle required, place level in plumb position, Illus. 142, and draw a line.

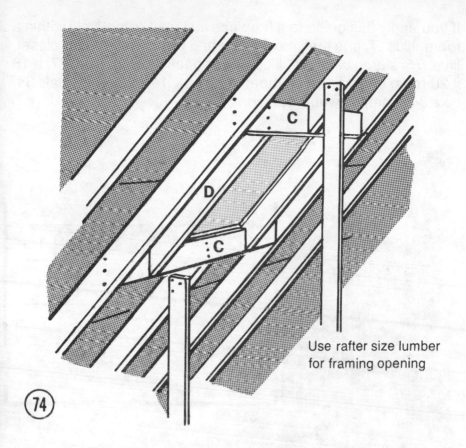

Use rafter size lumber
for framing opening

74

You can now remove 2 x 4 bracing.

Your home improvement retailer supplies a complete package—fireplaces with 24 to 48" screened openings; 6", 2' and 3' chimney sections that can be installed up to 49'9" in overall height; a fire resistant hearth, roof housings, etc. He does need to know what kind and size fireplace you want. The size will be determined by the overall size and height of the room, and where in the room it's to be placed. One way to zero in on size of opening is to add the width and length of the room. Use the total as a guide. For example: A room measuring 16 x 20 = 36. This room could accept a fireplace with a 36" opening, Illus. 6, 10.

If you apply this guide to a fireplace installed completely within a room, Illus. 7, one that may be finished with a wall-to-wall closet, Illus. 75; stereo cabinets, Illus. 76, or bookshelves, Illus. 77, a 16 x 20 room could finish up measuring only 14 x 20. This totals 34, so a 34" opening would suffice.

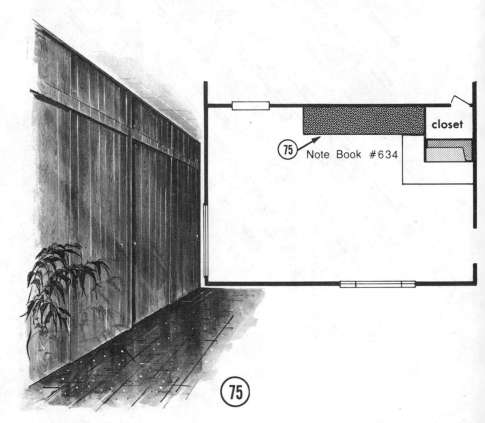

There are other factors that must be considered. If outside walls aren't insulated, or the room contains windows facing prevailing winds, or the room has 8'6" or 9'0" ceilings, your retailer could logically suggest a 36" fireplace.

A wood burning fireplace needs lots and lots of air. If ceiling height is 7'0" or 7'6", and the room is filled with furniture, a 28 or 30" opening may be all you need even though the overall total, width plus length equals 36. If the room is in a warm part of the house, and insulated glass or storm windows seal out winter winds, a smaller opening would be recommended. Also

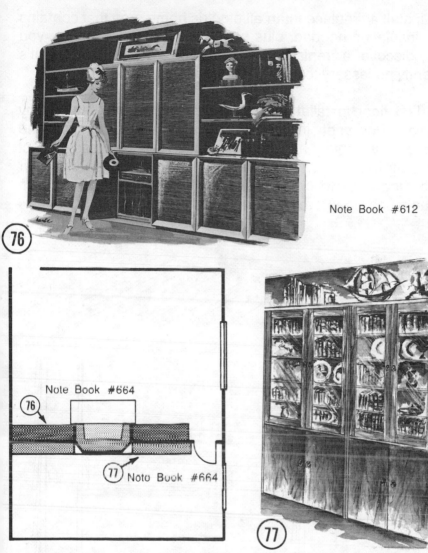

Note Book #612

Note Book #664

76

77 Note Book #664

76

77

consider future improvements. Will the room selected for a fireplace be modernized with wall-to-wall closets, or expanded by opening up a wall? Do future plans include an oversized couch or chairs? The size of a room and the contents are important when selecting size of fireplace opening. Also consider the availability of logs in size the firplace needs to burn most effectively. A 28" opening will burn 18 to 20" logs while a 36" opening will take 24 to 26". Unless the room has sufficient cubage, the fire will need to draw air from a hall, stairway, or other rooms.

If you install a fireplace in an all electric home, one that contains all the insulation needed, plus storm or insulated windows, you quickly discover a fireplace needs lots of oxygen. In this case it's frequently necessary to provide more air to the fireplace room.

On a first floor installation, additional air can be obtained by cutting a narrow vent* in the floor, or wall, Illus. 78, alongside the fireplace. This could draw air from a basement, or a cold air duct can pull air from an adjacent room. Use a hot air heating or air conditioning grille to cover opening. This permits a hot fire to draw as much air as it requires.

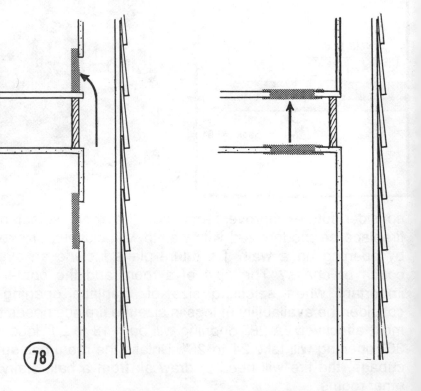

*Vent opening should equal size of flue.

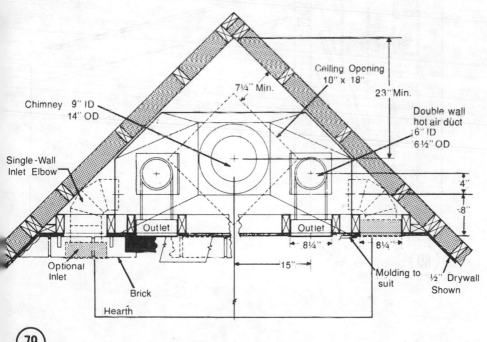

(78)

Make and test the fireplace without this vent. If the fireplace smokes, or pulls air from a hall or stairway, install one vent. In some well insulated houses, two vents, one on each side of the fireplace are needed. Install grilles close to, or in front of fireplace. Use grilles that can be closed when fireplace is not being used.

If you install a fireplace across a corner, Illus. 79, or use it as a room divider, Illus. 4, consider how it will necessitate moving furniture.

Ceiling Opening
10" x 18"

7¼" Min.

23" Min.

Chimney 9" ID
14" OD

Double wall
hot air duct
6" ID
6½" OD

Single-Wall
Inlet Elbow

4"

8"

Outlet

Outlet

8¼"

8¼"

Optional
Inlet

15"

Molding to
suit

½" Drywall
Shown

Brick

Hearth

(79)

Where you position a fireplace dictates location of the chimney. Since this must exit roof and project 3' above roof, or 2' above any portion of roof within 10', Illus. 80; the search for the best location can start in the fireplace room or in the attic.

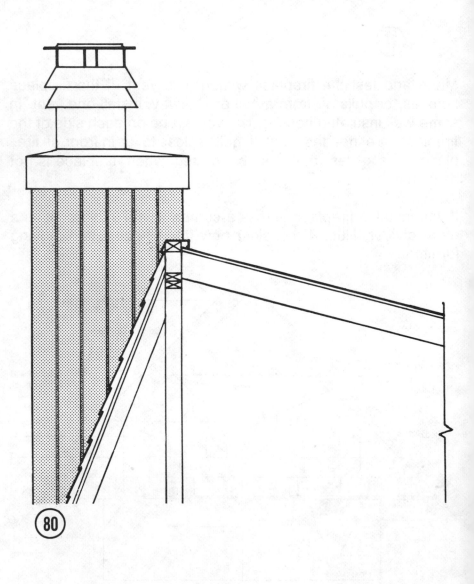

80

CONTEMPORARY CHIMNEY CAP

Illus. 81 shows a contemporary cap and storm collar that is frequently installed on vacation homes and on top of housings erected on flat roofs, Illus. 182. The cone is marked to indicate various roof pitches. This simplifies cutting cone to pitch of roof.

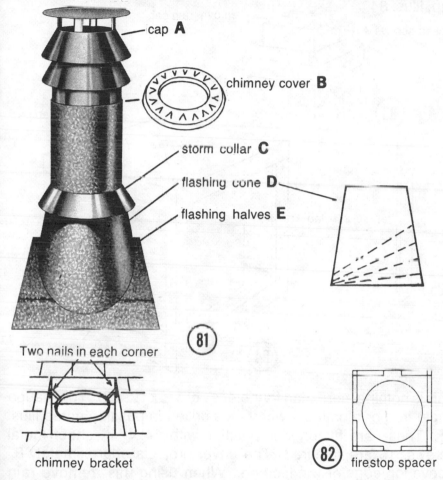

cap **A**

chimney cover **B**

storm collar **C**

flashing cone **D**

flashing halves **E**

(81)

Two nails in each corner

chimney bracket

(82) firestop spacer

Since a chimney section only weighs 12 lbs. per foot, and the firestop, Illus. 82, and all other components are sheet metal, the entire job can be done by one person. The only place where help is needed is in positioning the fireplace unit on the floor, and in positioning a chimney housing with flashing attached. Two people working on the roof simplifies positioning housing and lessens damage to shingles.

WIND CAP

If your house is located in a low area, or surrounded by tall trees, or higher buildings, natural air currents frequently create a downdraft in the chimney. In this case, loosen screws A, Illus. 83. DO NOT REMOVE SCREWS. Lift up rain cap, install a wind cap, Illus. 84.

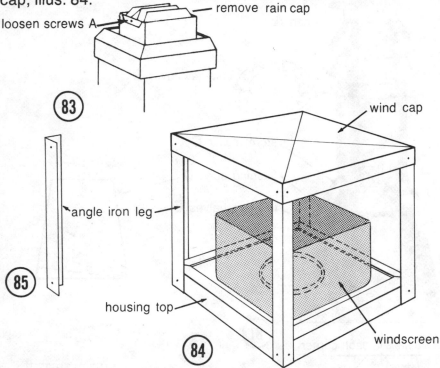

remove rain cap

loosen screws A

wind cap

angle iron leg

housing top

windscreen

This is nothing more than four pieces of 1½ x 1½ x 27" light gauge angle iron or aluminum with holes drilled in position noted, Illus. 85. These are fastened in position with 14 x ¼" sheet metal screws, 16 are required. The cover projects approximately 8" above top edge of windscreen. When using this, remove rain cap furnished with housing.

The wind cap helps eliminate a downdraft just as ample air within the fireplace room helps insure a free burning fire. Buy angle iron and have a metal cap fabricated locally. Use aluminum angle and cap if housing is aluminum; use steel angle iron with a tin cap if housing is tin.

BRACING FLOOR JOISTS

While the manufacturer recommends installing these metal fireplaces on a finished floor, and doesn't specify additional floor framing, the author recommends nailing solid bridging, Illus. 86, under perimeter of fireplace and hearth. This helps eliminate any movement by a jovial crowd. It also helps prevent settling in an older house.

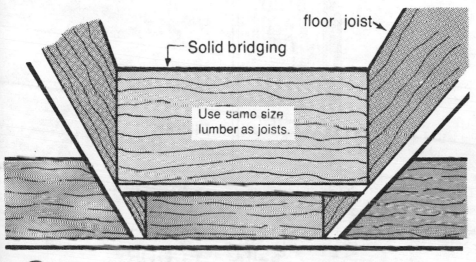

If a floor slopes, or gives at any one point when a heavy person walks over, all spring in floor should be eliminated. This can be done in several ways.

First examine joists. Test with a knife to see if there's any dry rot. Note where joist rests on bedplate, Illus. 87, or on foundation.

If joist contains dry rot, termites, etc., take the load off joists by jacking up those damaged. Raise only to level position, Illus. 88. Using same size lumber, bolt a joist three times the length of the damaged area to existing joist. Drill holes and bolt two joists together. Use a length of lumber that sets on bedplate or foundation and extends at least four feet beyond rotted section,

Illus. 89. If joists, when jacked up level, don't set solidly on foundation, flush cement mortar consisting of one part cement to three parts of screened sand under ends of new joists. Allow mortar to set three days before removing jacks.

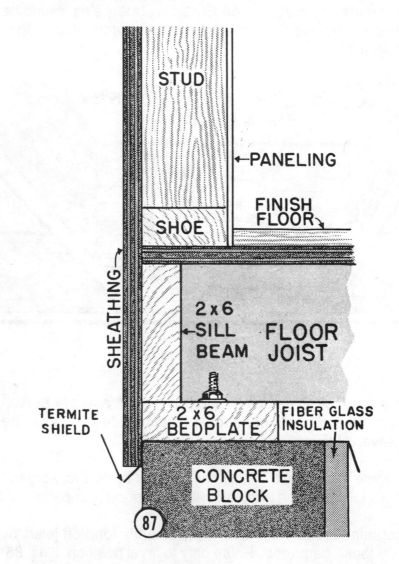

STUD

PANELING

FINISH FLOOR

SHOE

SHEATHING

2 x 6 SILL BEAM

FLOOR JOIST

TERMITE SHIELD

2 x 6 BEDPLATE

FIBER GLASS INSULATION

CONCRETE BLOCK

87

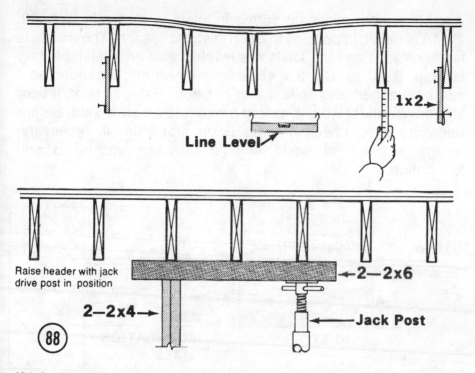

1x2

Line Level

Raise header with jack drive post in position

2—2x6

2—2x4

Jack Post

(88)

If joists appear solid, you can usually eliminate movement with solid bridging, Illus. 86. Use lumber same size as floor joist. Spike joists to bridging with 16 or 20 penny nails. Stagger bridging slightly to permit nailing through joists into bridging. Install bridging wherever weakness requires same.

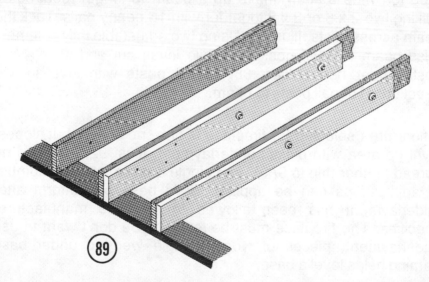

(89)

Another way to eliminate spring in joists is shown in Illus. 90. 2 x 4A is nailed in position to each joist in question. The weight is taken off joist and the joists are leveled with an adjustable lally column, Illus. 88. Cut 2 x 4B to length and angle needed so it can be wedged and spiked into position. Remove jack. If floor still moves under weight, repeat procedure on other side. Before releasing jack, check bracing B on first side. If necessary, wedge a piece of wood shingle between end of B and foundation.

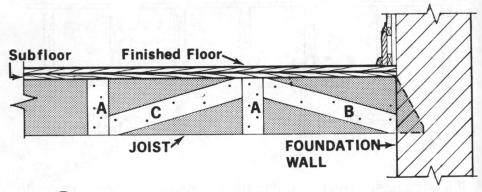

Subfloor   Finished Floor

A   C   A   B

JOIST   FOUNDATION WALL

If you happen to own a house with undersize floor joists, i.e., 2 x 6 on too wide a span, make up a beam to length required by spiking two 2 x 6 or 2 x 8 together with 16 penny nails. Tack the beam across joists, Illus. 91. Using two adjustable lally columns, raise beam to level position. While level, cut and drive 4 x 4 posts under beam, Illus. 88. Check posts with level in two directions. Toenail posts to beam.

If floor area selected for fireplace is firm, no spring, but slopes, level up area with plastic underlayment, Illus. 92. This can be spread feather thin to 5/16" in a single application. Any number of applications can be applied. Build base or platform after underlayment has been allowed to set time manufacturer specifies. The fireplace must be level. If you don't want to use underlayment, pieces of wood shingle wedged under base framing helps level a base.

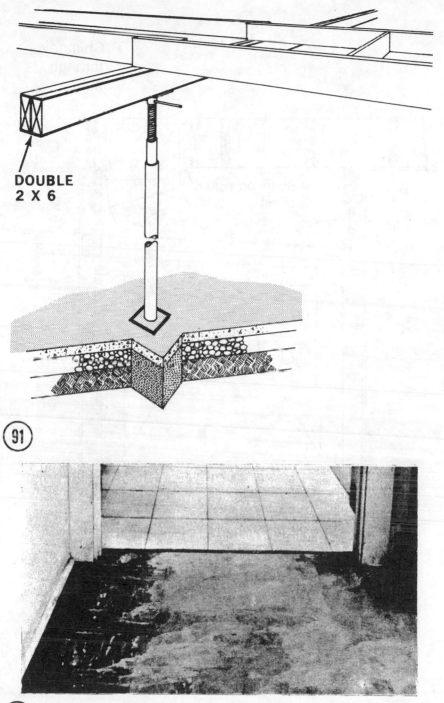

DOUBLE 2 X 6

(91)

(92)

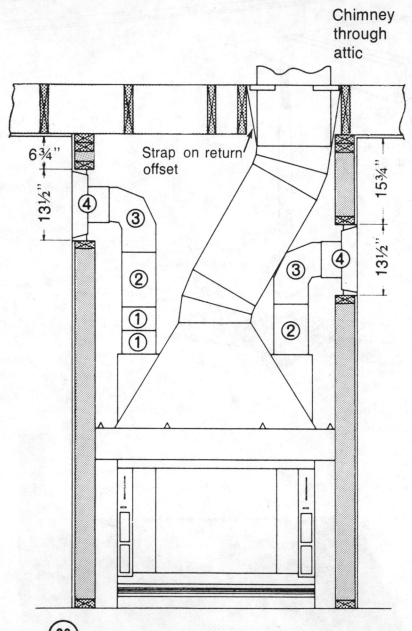

Chimney through attic

Strap on return offset

6¾"

13½"

15¾"

13½"

④ ③ ② ① ①

③ ④ ②

⑨③

72

Installing a fireplace follows this general procedure, note Illus. 1. The fireplace is placed on the finished floor, or on a raised base in position that permits installing a chimney straight up, or angled to the back, right or left.

If the chimney is to be installed straight up, the starter section, provided by manufacturer, is fastened in position indicated with screws provided, Illus. 47.

Always read and follow directions packed with each component. Due to material or design changes the manufacturer is not responsible unless installation of each part follows his directions.

When you unpack the fireplace, check the damper to see if it operates freely. Check it again when fireplace is placed in position and again after all framing has been nailed in place and chimney installed.

Before moving fireplace into position, cover the damper to prevent any debris from falling in. This is vitally important since even a small piece of plaster can cause lots of trouble.

If the chimney is to be angled, a starter offset, either 15°, Illus. 48, or 30°, Illus. 49, is twist locked to starter section then fastened with screws manufacturer provides. Offsets are always installed in the room with fireplace, Illus. 93. Straps on return offset, Illus. 48, are nailed to header and joists around opening, Illus. 94.

The return offset must be twist locked to top of starter section, or to a 6", 2' or 3' chimney section, or any combination of sections can be fastened to the chimney starter section. The return offset is then twist locked to the top. In every case, use the holes in the return offset to drill holes in chimney section.

Elbows, Illus. 95, are always installed above fireplace room, Illus. 96. Complete details covering use of elbows are explained on page 86.

FRAMING FOR CHIMNEY

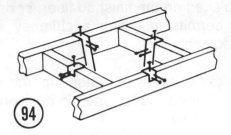

94

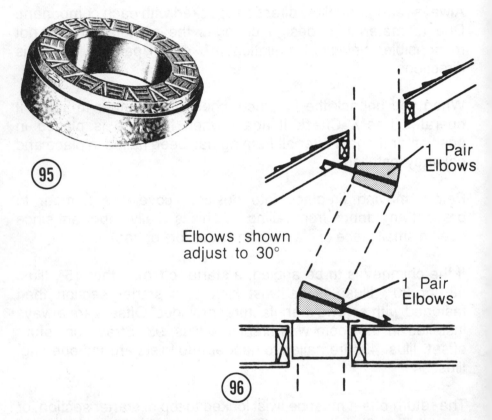

95

1 Pair
Elbows

Elbows shown
adjust to 30°

1 Pair
Elbows

96

Illus. 97 shows a typical 30° offset installation. Note straps on return offset, Illus. 48, are fastened to headers and joists in opening, Illus. 94. When estimating what you need and where each component is to be installed, check overall dimensions A, B, C & D, Illus. 97, 1.

When corbeling a chimney for a 15° incline, the starter offset is fastened to the bottom of the starter section, Illus. 48.

74

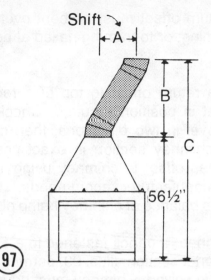

Shift

←A→

B

C

56½"

(97)

The assembled unit is then fastened to the fireplace, Illus. 98, in position that angles chimney 15° to the back, front, or to right or left. The return offset is fastened to top of the starter section, or to the top of a chimney section. This can be a 6", 2' or 3' section. Use size required.

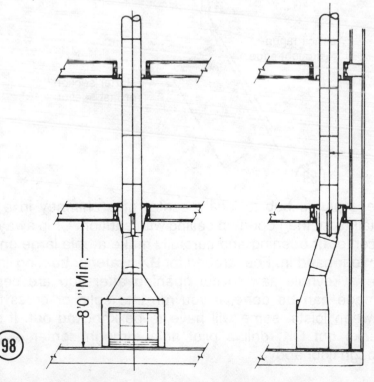

8'0" Min.

(98)

The straps on a return offset must be bent over and nailed to framing around opening; or to framing nailed at height required. Use 8 penny nails.

When you mount a return offset to top of a regular chimney section, place offset in position required. Check with level to make certain it's level in two directions, then drill four 1/16" diameter holes in chimney section in exact position holes in offset indicate. Fasten offset to chimney using 1" sheet metal screws, or screws manufacturer recommends. The offset must be level. This insures balance of chimney being plumb.

As previously described, a pencil fastened to a 1 x 3" x 3', Illus. 67, placed on the starter section, Illus. 99, permits marking exact position of opening in ceiling. Chimney must have 2" clearance all around as it goes through each floor. The opening in each floor above fireplace must be framed to allow this 2" clearance.

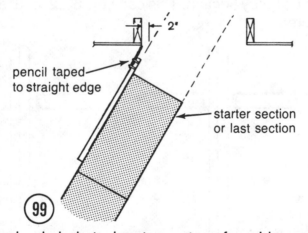

pencil taped to straight edge

2"

starter section or last section

99

Use a plumb bob to locate center of a chimney in a vertical installation, then open up ceiling with caution. Chip away plaster at center of opening and carefully make a hole large enough to put your hand in. Feel around for BX, water or heating lines, etc. Use a keyhole saw to cut opening after you are certain no damage can be done. If you run into solid or cross bridging between joists, same will have to be knocked out. If opening checks out OK, drill a pilot hole through center of opening through floor above.

A 7" flue vertical installation requires cutting joist A, Illus. 100, 18½" for a 15½ x 15½" opening.

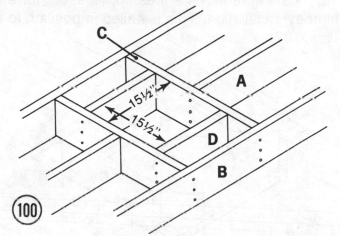

Cut joist A 21" for a 9" chimney—vertical installation. This permits nailing framing 18 x 18", Illus. 101. This framing provides 2" space needed all around flue. If necessary, cut opening in ceiling oversize to simplify installing C and D. In some cases you may only need one D and two C. Spike through C into A. Nail B to C, through C into D, or where this isn't possible toenail D to C. In every case nail down through floor above into A, C and D. Use same size lumber as A for C and D.

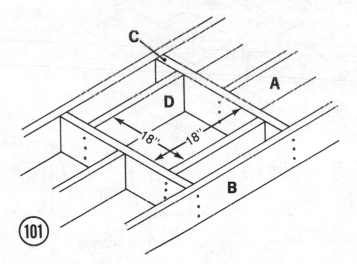

FIRESTOP SPACERS

An 18 x 18" opening requires a firestop, Illus. 82, for a 9" flue vertical chimney installation. This is nailed in position to bottom opening. Illus. 102.

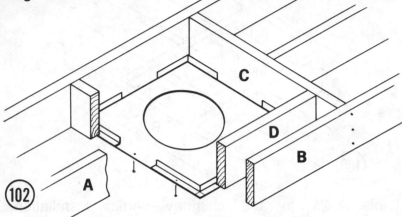

If a 15° offset is installed, Illus. 48, frame opening 18 x 21⅝" for a 9" flue, Illus. 103. This requires firestop, Illus. 104, nailed to bottom of opening.

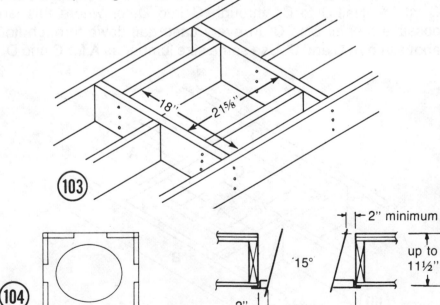

Illus. 105 shows opening in a floor measuring up to 11½" in overall thickness. This is for a 9" flue corbeled to 15°.

Illus. 106 indicates an 18 x 26⅞" opening for a 9" flue angled at 30°. This requires the firestop shown in Illus. 107, nailed to bottom of opening, Illus. 102, through a ceiling and floor 11½" in overall thickness.

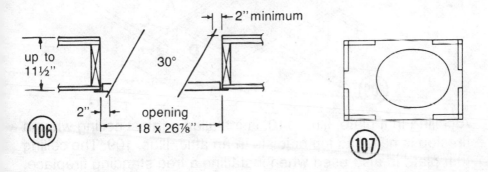

Illus. 108 shows an 18 x 21⅝" or 18 x 26⅞" opening for a 9" flue with a 30° incline through a ceiling and floor measuring more than 11½" in thickness. Note 2 x 4 nailed in position. While a longer opening is required, a 2 x 4 nailed in position shown maintains a 2" clearance. This permits nailing firestop. Always nail headers or framing in position required to anchor straps on a return offset, but never closer than 2".

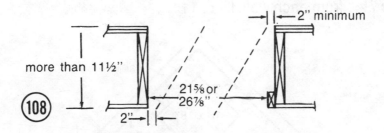

As you go through each floor, the firestop spacer must be installed in position indicated to bottom of joists. Drive 4 penny nails through each lip. The exception occurs when chimney goes through attic floor. In this case the firestop is nailed to top of joists, Illus. 109.

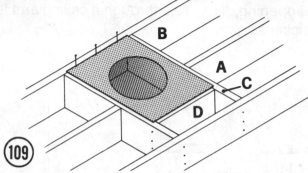

A ceiling trim plate, Illus. 110, is installed against ceiling when a firestop is nailed to top of joists in an attic, Illus. 109. The ceiling trim plate is also used when installing a free standing fireplace, Illus. 5, 321, 329.

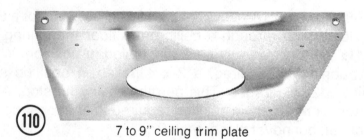

7 to 9" ceiling trim plate

Illus. 79 shows a fireplace in a corner installation. The 18 x 18" opening for chimney must be framed in position required. This will be 7¼" from each wall, Illus. 111.

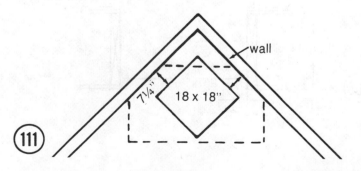

80

As previously mentioned, an outside wall must be insulated to permit the fireplace to work to greatest efficiency. If you don't want to remove existing lathe and plaster, drill holes and blow in loose insulation. This should be done by a commercial insulating company. Or you can nail 2 x 2's, 16" on centers, and staple aluminum foil covered rock wool batts to 2 x 2 within area enclosed by fireplace framing. Place unit in position and double check to make certain it's centered and elbows clear side walls. Install 6" single wall elbows in air intake openings; 6½" insulated elbows to hot air outlets. You don't need the 6" single wall elbows if you use cold air inlets on front, Illus. 10.

Illus. 112 shows opening in ceiling for a vertical chimney when fireplace is installed against a wall.

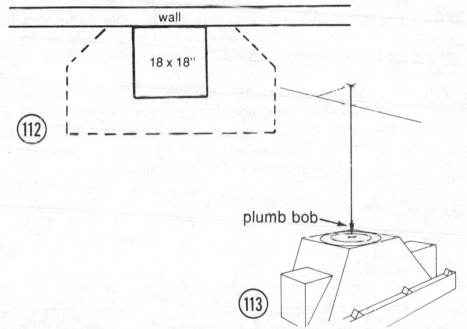

wall

18 x 18"

(112)

plumb bob

(113)

After placing unit in position, place starter chimney section in position. To locate opening for a vertical flue, use the 1 x 3" x 3', Illus. 67, to draw opening on ceiling, or drop a plumb bob, Illus. 113, down from ceiling to center of flue, Illus. 114. Since a lathe and plaster ceiling may contain metal or wood lathe, use a blade that cuts through metal.

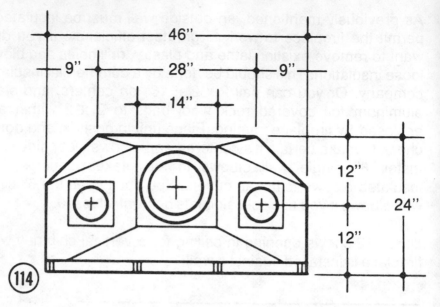

(114)

When you open up the ceiling, you will be able to determine direction and spacing between joists. Make opening large enough to permit nailing headers D in position, Illus. 101.

Note overall dimensions of a 36" fireplace, Illus. 115. The overall depth of unit is 24". The outside dimension of a chimney is 14". The chimney sets 2" from back of unit. If you remove a shoe molding and place the unit against a baseboard, the overall distance from wall to chimney will be approximately 3".

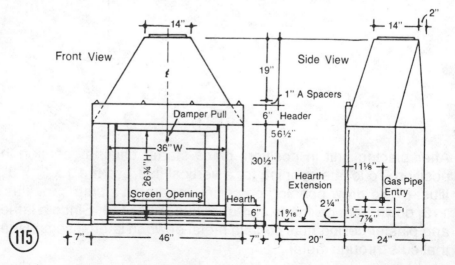

(115)

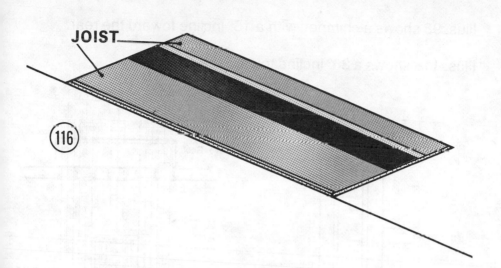

JOIST

(116)

If joists in ceiling run parallel to wall, Illus. 116, you might be able to frame opening as shown in Illus. 117. Headers C and D, Illus. 102, reinforce cut joist.

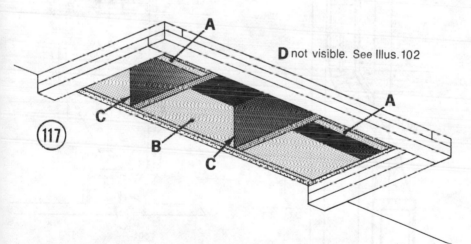

A

D not visible. See Illus. 102

A

(117)

C

B

C

After framing in opening to size specified, nail floor to C and D with 10 penny nails. Place firestop through a section of chimney so it can be nailed in position recommended with 8 penny nails.

To more fully appreciate how you can install a chimney where it doesn't create problems passing through a second floor and attic, consider the many alternatives.

Illus. 98 shows a chimney with a 15° incline toward the rear.

Illus. 118 shows a 30° incline toward the rear.

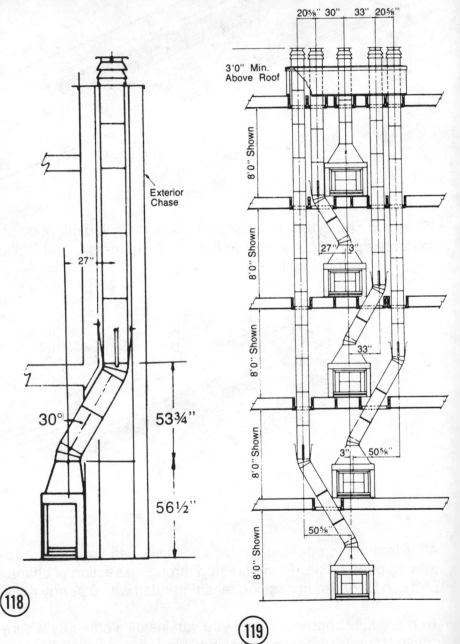

Illus. 119 shows a 30° incline to the right or left.

Illus. 120 shows fireplaces in adjacent rooms served by two chimneys with a 15° offset to the right.

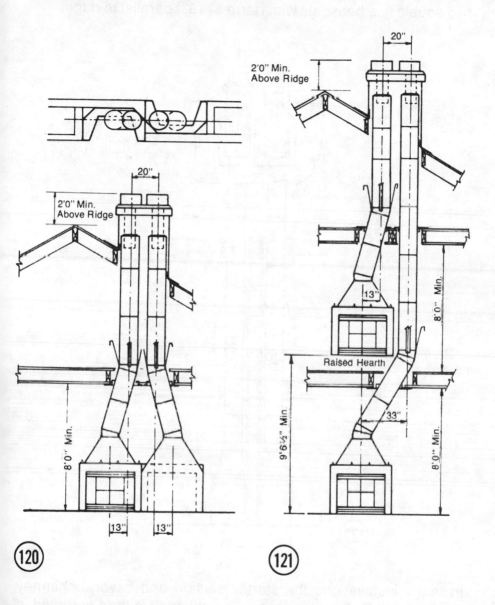

Illus. 121 shows installation of fireplaces on two floors. The lower fireplace uses a 30° offset while the chimney serving the fireplace on the floor above uses a 15° offset. Note how one chimney housing surrounds two flues.

Illus. 122 shows four fireplaces in adjacent rooms on two floors. Positioned 9" apart, back to back, the four flues exit roof within two double flue housings with narrow (18") parallel to ridge.

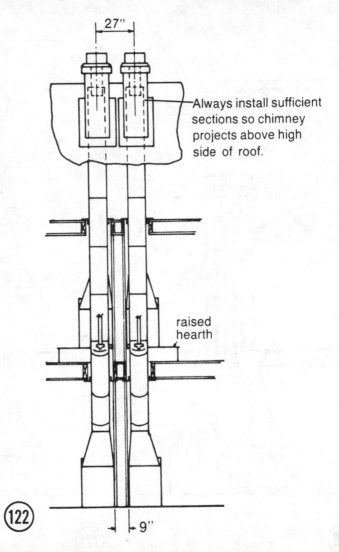

27"

Always install sufficient sections so chimney projects above high side of roof.

raised hearth

(122)

9"

In many installations the starter section and several chimney sections are fastened in place. The chimney is then corbeled in direction needed above the fireplace room, Illus. 96. In this case elbows, Illus. 95, are used instead of offsets. Elbows twist lock to a chimney section. Elbows are adjustable from 0 to 30° and are used only outside the room containing the fireplace.

Elbows in pairs can be adjusted to provide any angle from 5° incline to 30° as shown, Illus. 123. This chart indicates the various angles that can be achieved with two pair of adjustable elbows, plus 2' or 3' chimney sections. If only one pair of elbows is used, chimney inclines 15°. For any other angle, two pairs must be used.

INCLINED CHIMNEYS AT VARIOUS ANGLES*

(Using 0 - 30° Adjustable Elbows -- See Elbow Text)

	Each 2' Chim. Sec.		Each 3' Chim. Sec.	
	Adds To Shift	Adds To Ht.	Adds To Shift	Adds To Ht.
5° Incline	2"	23 1/8"	3 1/16"	35 1/16"
10° Incline	4 1/16"	22 7/8"	6 1/8"	34 11/16"
15° Incline	6"	22 7/16"	9 1/8"	14"
20° Incline	8"	21 13/16"	12 1/16"	33 1/8"
25° Incline	9 7/8"	21 1/16"	14 7/8"	11 15/16"
30° (Max.) Incline	11 5/8"	20 1/8"	17 5/8"	30 1/2"

(123)

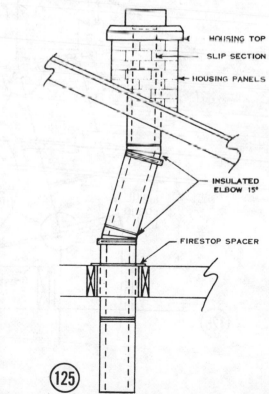

HOUSING TOP

SLIP SECTION

HOUSING PANELS

INSULATED ELBOW 15°

FIRESTOP SPACER

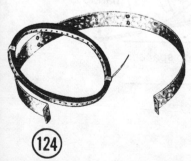

(124)

(125)

*Specifications provided by manufacturer.

Elbows are packed in pairs with two joint bands, Illus. 124, and a 20' coil of support strap.

When a fixed 15° angle is needed, use one elbow per bend, Illus. 125. In an attic installation, the firestop spacer is nailed to top of joists.

Joint bands are fastened around chimney, Illus. 126. Sight align holes in joint band over center of joint. Only hand tighten bolts holding band in position. Tap each lug with a hammer, then tighten bolts holding joint band. Straps, wrapped around chimney and nailed to framing, provide additional support.

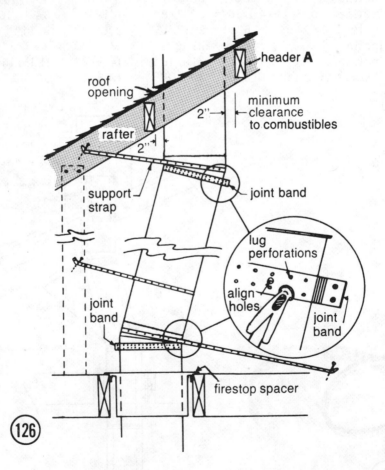

RATIO OF HEIGHT - SLOPE - SHIFT

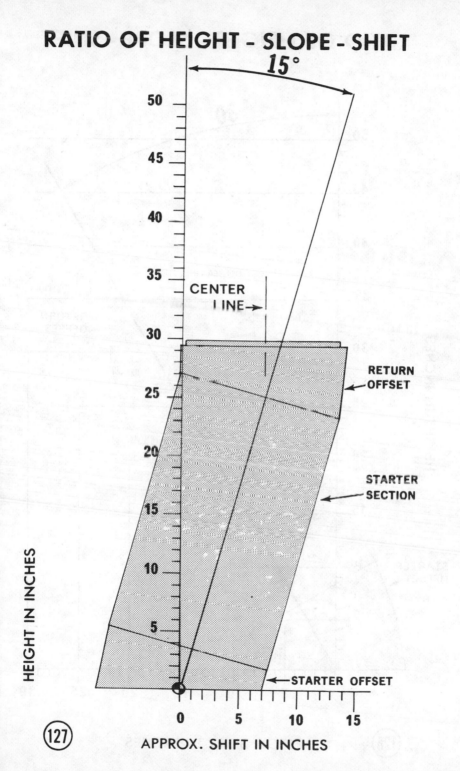

15°

50

45

40

35

CENTER
LINE

30

RETURN
OFFSET

25

20

STARTER
SECTION

15

10

5

HEIGHT IN INCHES

STARTER OFFSET

0   5   10   15

⑫⑦

APPROX. SHIFT IN INCHES

RATIO OF HEIGHT - SLOPE - SHIFT

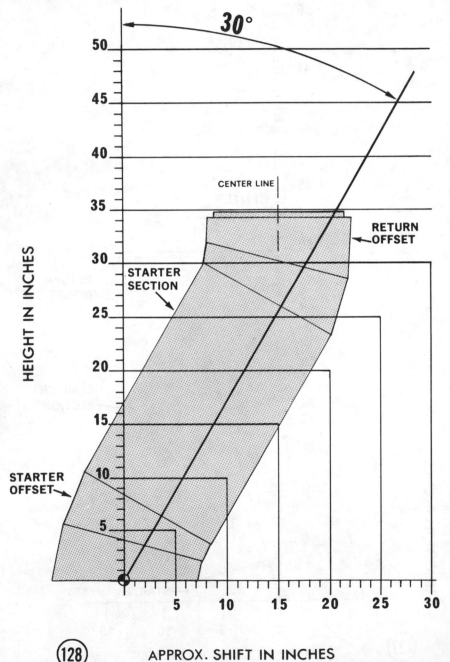

HEIGHT IN INCHES

30°

CENTER LINE

RETURN OFFSET

STARTER SECTION

STARTER OFFSET

APPROX. SHIFT IN INCHES

Lower ends of elbow are not threaded. This permits 360° rotation to desired direction. As previously mentioned, elbows are always installed above fireplace room while offsets are used in the fireplace room.

Illus. 127 shows distance of shift at various points for a chimney inclined at 15°.

Illus. 128 shows distance of shift at various points for a chimney inclined at 30°.

Illus. 129 shows amount of shift for a 15° and 30° offset using the starter section and a 2' or 3' chimney section.

USE OF 15° & 30° OFFSETS*

	"A" Total Shift	"B" Ht. From Top of Fireplace to top of the Support Offset	"C" Ht. From Bottom of Fireplace to Top of Offset (Nearest Inch)
15°			
*Offset used alone	1"	30 1/4"	7' 3"
Off. & St. Sec.	7"	29 1/2"	7' 2"
Off. & St. Sec. + One 2' Chim.	13"	51 3/4"	9' 0"
Off. & St. Sec. + One 3' Chim.	16"	63 1/4"	10' 0"
Off. & St. Sec. + Two 2' Chim.	19"	74"	10'10"
Off. & St. Sec. + One 2' Chim. + One 3' Chim.	22"	85 3/4"	11'10"
Off. & St. Sec + Two 3' Chim.	25"	97 1/4"	12'10"
30°			
*Offset used Alone	4"	37"	7' 9"
Off. & St. Sec	15"	33 3/4"	7' 6"
Off. & St. Sec. + One 2' Chim	27"	53 3/4"	9' 2"
Off. & St. Sec. + One 3' Chim.	33"	64"	10' 1"
Off. & St. Sec. + Two 2' Chim.	39"	73 3/4"	10'10"
Off. & St. Sec. + One 2' Chim. + One 3' Chim.	45"	84 1/4"	11' 9"
Off. & St. Sec. + Two 3' Chim.	51"	94 1/2"	12' 7"

* On top of vertically-installed Starter Section.

(129)

*Specifications provided by manufacturer.

Where distance between offsets or elbows exceeds 9 feet, anchor support straps to studs. Always maintain a minimum of 2" between chimney and framing throughout its entire length.

Illus. 130 indicates height limitations of a vertical prefabricated chimney supported by a fireplace. Allowing 54" for fireplace, 2' for starter section, you can install a chimney to an overall height of 49'9".

VERTICAL INSTALLATION HT. TO CHIMNEY TOP*
RADIANT HEAT UNIT, Illus.6

Includes the Fireplace, 2'
Start. Sec., and
Chim. Sec. Shown

2 ft. Sec.	3 ft. Sec.	Height	2 ft. Sec.	3 ft. Sec.	Height
1	0	8' 7"	0	8	30'2"
0	1	9' 7"	2	7	31'1"
2	0	10' 6"	1	8	32'1"
1	1	11' 6"	0	9	33'1"
0	2	12'6"	2	8	34'0"
2	1	13'5"	1	9	35'0"
1	2	14'5"	0	10	36'0"
0	3	15'5"	2	9	37'0"
2	2	16'5"	1	10	38'0"
1	3	17'5"	0	11	39'0"
0	4	18'5"	2	10	39'11"
2	3	19'4"	1	11	40'11"
1	4	20'4"	0	12	41'11"
0	5	21'4"	2	11	42'10"
2	4	22'3"	1	12	43'10"
1	5	23'3"	0	13	44'10"
0	6	24'3"	2	12	45'9"
2	5	25'2"	1	13	46'9"
1	6	26'2"	0	14	47'9"
0	7	27'2"	2	13	48'9"
2	6	28'2"	1	14	49'9"
1	7	29'2"		See Ht. Limitations Above	

(130)

*Specifications provided by manufacturer.

The radiant and hot air fireplaces, Illus. 6, 10, come with a 2 or 3' starter section. When a chimney offset is installed, the height of chimney supported by offset should not exceed 47', Illus. 131.

HT.-CHIMNEY ONLY*
RADIANT HEAT UNIT, Illus. 6

2 ft. Sec.	3 ft. Sec.	Height	2 ft. Sec.	3 ft. Sec.	Height
1	0	1'11"	1	8	25'5"
0	1	2'11"	0	9	26'5"
2	0	3'10"	2	8	27'4"
1	1	4'10"	1	9	28'4"
0	2	5'10"	0	10	29'4"
2	1	6'10"	2	9	30'4"
1	2	7'10"	1	10	31'4"
0	3	8'10"	0	11	32'4"
2	2	9'9"	2	10	33'3"
1	3	10'9"	1	11	34'3"
0	4	11'9"	0	12	35'3"
2	3	12'8"	2	11	36'2"
1	4	13'8"	1	12	37'2"
0	5	14'8"	0	13	38'2"
2	4	15'7"	2	12	39'1"
1	5	16'7"	1	13	40'1"
0	6	17'7"	0	14	41'1"
2	5	18'7"	2	13	42'1"
1	6	19'7"	1	14	43'1"
0	7	20'7"	0	15	44'1"
2	6	21'6"	2	14	45'0"
1	7	22'6"	1	15	46'0"
0	8	23'6"	0	16	47'0"
2	7	24'5"			

(131)

(*Does NOT include starter section)

OPENING IN ROOF

To estimate the number of 6", 2' and 3' sections of chimney, and/or offsets or elbows, your supplier will need to know the ceiling height of each room, thickness of each floor, and height above roof, Illus. 1.

The opening in a pitched roof is framed as shown, Illus. 74.

Since a good part of the total installation can be done before you need to open up the roof, plan this part of the work when the weather is clear, the chance for rain is nil, and there's no wind. But play safe. Get a large piece of heavy polyethylene or canvas, some 1 x 2 and a stapling gun. Roll a couple of inches of polyethylene on the 1 x 2 and staple in place. Temporarily nail the 1 x 2 to the roof, Illus. 132. Use this as a cover after you open up the roof.

To locate center of a chimney, drop a plumb bob down from roof sheathing and mark center on sheathing, Illus. 133. Drive a nail through sheathing to indicate center of flue, Illus. 134.

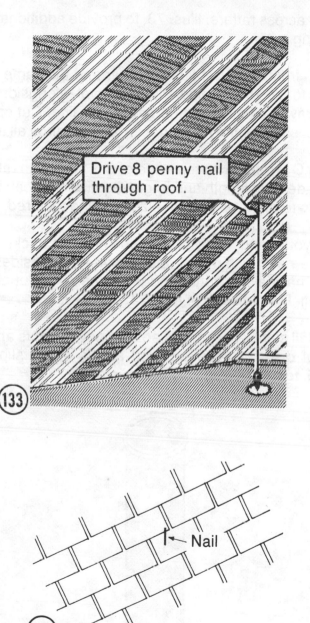

Drive 8 penny nail through roof.

(133)

Nail

(134)

Draw outline for opening. A 7" flue requires a 15½ x 15½" opening ; a 9" flue requires 18 x 18". Use rafter size lumber for framing C and D.

Nail a 2 x 4 across rafters, Illus. 73, to provide additional support before cutting rafter.

Measure 9" from center of flue up rafter and the same distance down rafter for an 18" opening. Plumb a level[1] alongside rafter A, Illus. 73. Draw a plumb line and saw along line. Cut opening in roof to exact size chimney requires for 2" clearance all around.

Nail header C to rafter A so top edge of C is flush with rafter, Illus. 74. Cut header D to length and angle required so it can be nailed in position to form an 18 x 18" or size opening required.

To protect your hand, apply tape to one end of a hacksaw blade. Saw shingle nails*within 5"of opening on top and sides. Do not cut shingle nails along bottom edge of opening. Cut nails flush with #15 felt. Don't disturb or tear #15 felt.

Always install sufficient sections so chimney projects above high side of roof distance required, and allows a 32" slip section, Illus. 1, 135, to be inserted 2" or more into flue.

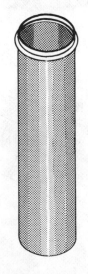

(135)

1- Note Illus. 142.
* or rent a nail cutter, Illus.148

CHIMNEY HOUSING

A single chimney housing, Illus. 1, 136, measuring 18 x 18" x 3'0", or 18 x 18" x 5'0", plus the slip section, automatically increases overall height of a flue above roof, even after cutting housing to pitch of roof.

(136)

A double chimney housing, Illus. 137, requires an 18 x 38" opening. When installing a double housing decide whether the long or short side is to be parallel to ridge. Frame opening so center of flue is 9" from ends. This places center of flues 20" apart, Illus. 138. If necessary use 15° or 30° elbows to obtain this spacing.

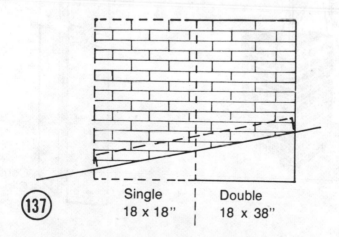

(137)   Single   Double
        18 x 18"   18 x 38"

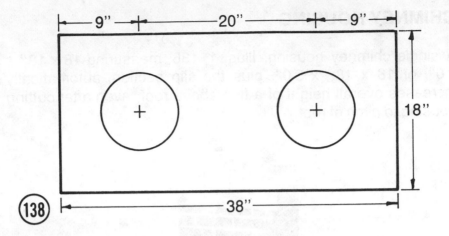

(138)

The chimney housing is available KD in 3 and 5' heights for both single or double flue. The housing should extend at least 3' above the high side where it comes through roof. Since the raincap adds almost 12" to overall height, what you lose when cutting housing to pitch of roof, you gain with a raincap or wind cap.

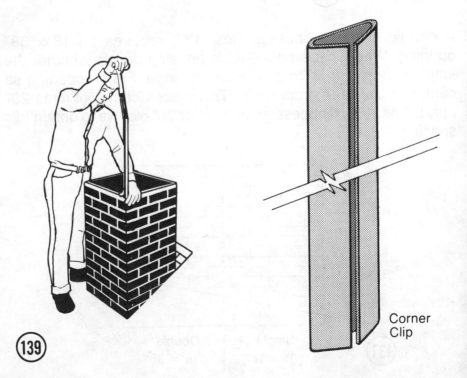

(139)

Corner Clip

98

The chimney housing must be cut on the job to pitch of roof. First decide whether long side of a double housing, or short side, is to be parallel to ridge. Let's assume long side will be parallel to ridge. Cut short side to pitch of pattern, Illus. 144.

To simplify cutting housing to exact pitch of your roof, do this. Working in the attic, thumbtack a piece of cardboard with a straight edge to a rafter, Illus. 140.

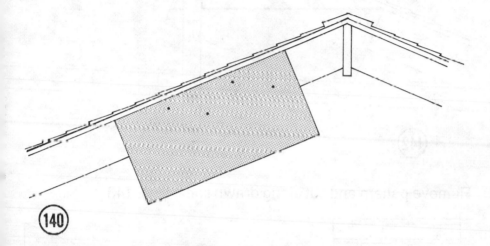

(140)

Place a level In horizontal position shown, Illus. 141. Draw a level line.

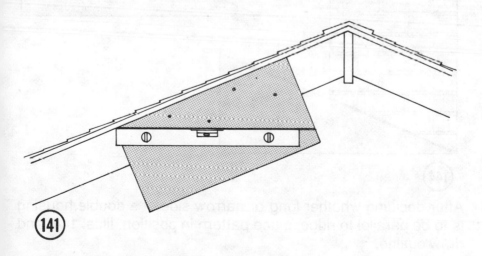

(141)

99

Place level in plumb position, Illus. 142, and draw a line.

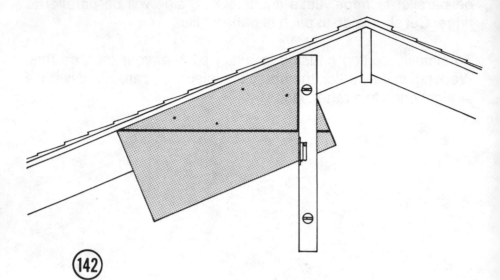

(142)

Remove pattern and cut along drawn lines, Illus. 143.

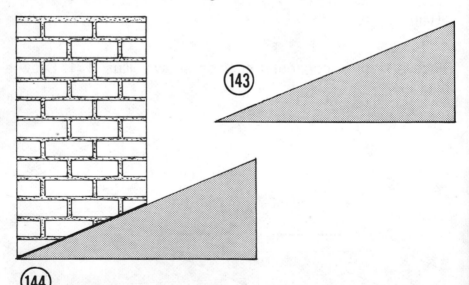

(143)

(144)

After deciding whether long or narrow side of a double housing is to be parallel to ridge, place pattern in position, Illus. 144, and draw outline.

Using a hacksaw or aviation snips, cut sides to angle of pattern, before assembling housing, Illus. 145, 146.

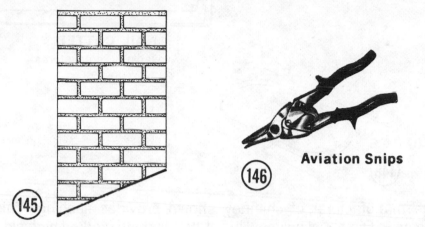

Aviation Snips

Use a straight edge and bend high side to shape shown, Illus. 147. This flange should not be less than 4".

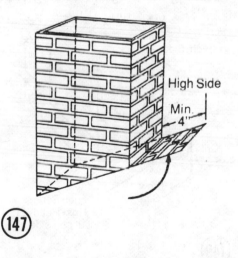

High Side

Min. 4"

Corners of housing panels are identical. Align corners and lock together with a sliding corner clip. Cut corner clips to length required on high side, Illus. 139. The 5' panels require two corner clips. One is inserted from top down, the other from bottom up. If you have to take housing apart, pull out fasteners with pliers.

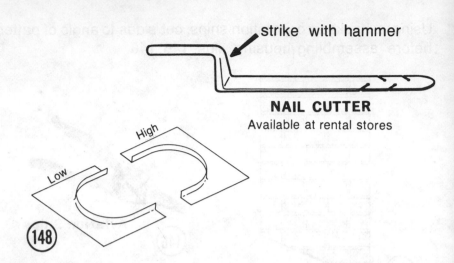

strike with hammer

NAIL CUTTER
Available at rental stores

High

Low

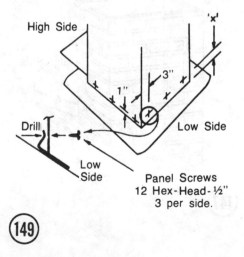
(148)

The manufacturer of chimney shown provides flashing. This comes in two equal halves, Illus. 148. Flashing marked high side overlaps flashing marked low side. Use asphalt cement to seal overlap. Fasten flashing to housing using sheet metal screws supplied by manufacturer. It's essential to follow manufacturer's directions when fastening flashing to housing, Illus. 149.

High Side

'x'

3"

1"

Drill

Low Side

Low
Side

Panel Screws
12 Hex-Head-½"
3 per side.

(149)

To accurately position housing, remove rain cap, Illus. 83, and insert slip section, Illus. 151. The rain cap is removed by only loosening screws at A. Do not remove screws.

102

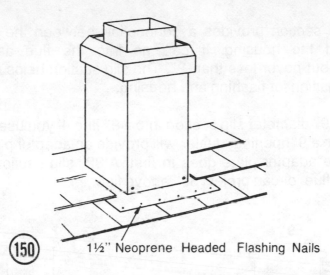

(150) 1½" Neoprene Headed Flashing Nails

With the aid of a helper, shingles on high and both sides of roof opening are raised and a bed of asphalt cement is spread over the #15 felt on roof. The lip on high side of housing and lips on both sides of flashing are slipped under shingles. The bottom flange on flashing is embedded in asphalt on TOP of existing shingles, Illus. 150.

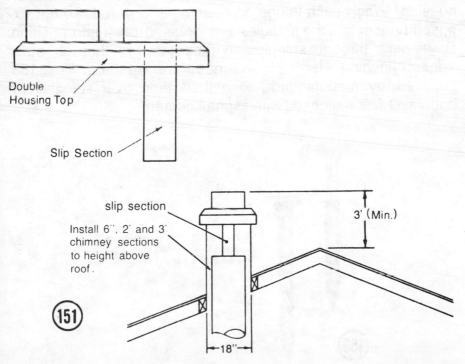

Double Housing Top

Slip Section

slip section

Install 6", 2' and 3' chimney sections to height above roof.

3' (Min.)

(151)

├──18"──┤

103

The slip section provides a connection between the chimney flue and the housing. It can go into the flue as far as needed but never less than 2". The slip section helps establish exact position for flashing and housing.

Install a 9" diameter slip section into a 9" flue. If you use a 7" slip section in a 9" opening, dealer will provide an adapter plate, Illus. 152. The adapter plate goes in first. A 32" slip section can go 30" into flue, or can project 30" above flue.

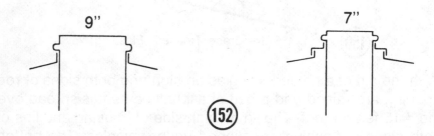

9"   7"

(152)

The shingles surrounding the housing are raised again and asphalt cement is applied over flashing and on top of lip on housing. When each flange on flashing is covered, except exposed bottom lip, the shingles are pressed back into position. Drive nails through shingles so they only go through outer edge of flashing. Use nails with neoprene washers, Illus. 153, supplied by manufacturer, to nail flashing over shingles on bottom. Cover nailheads with asphalt cement.

● The conical, resilient Neoprene washer plugs the nail hole "like the bung in a barrel."

(153)

104

Fasten corner brackets, Illus. 154, with bolts provided. Replace and fasten rain cap. Tighten nuts, Illus. 83.

(154)

If a wind cap, Illus. 84, is to be installed in place of the rain cap, drill holes through housing and fasten angle irons to four corners of housing. Position irons as shown. A sheet metal wind cap must be fabricated locally. This can be bolted to the angle irons with eight 1/4 or 5/16 x 1" bolts and nuts. After tightening nuts, use a screw driver and hammer to break a thread beside nut. This will prevent it from rattling loose in a high wind.

When installing two chimneys, plan same to exit roof 20" apart, center to center, Illus. 138. This allows 9" from center of flue to housing. Double check position of housing so it's squarely over opening and parallel to ridge. Remove raincap and insert slip sections. Follow procedure described for single flue housing. Nail through shingles into OUTER EDGE OF FLASHING. Use 1½" neoprene headed nails supplied with flashing. Use eight on long side, four on short side.

The Double Housing, Illus. 151, can also be used for a single chimney. In this installation fasten a Cover Cap over unused opening in top. Discard this cap whenever housing is installed over two flues.

PROTECTION AGAINST LIGHTNING

If your house is located on high ground and/or in an area subjected to lightning, ground the chimney. Run a lightning rod and ground cable fastened to a joint band, Illus. 124, or to a chimney bracket, Illus. 155, to a clamp fastened to a ½" x 4' iron reinforcing rod driven into ground. If your house is protected by lightning rods, or a grounded TV antenna that's close to and higher than your chimney, it should provide protection. To play safe, ground the chimney. Ask your fire insurance agent for information concerning company approved lightning protection. Follow their advice to insure getting complete coverage.

CHIMNEY INSTALLATION ON SIDE OF HOUSE

The chimney bracket is used to fasten chimney to exterior of house, Illus. 156. These brackets should be spaced every 9'. They should be nailed into studs. The bracket automatically spaces chimney 2" from house.

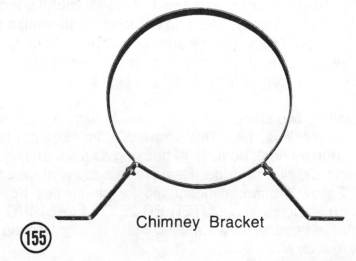

Chimney Bracket

155

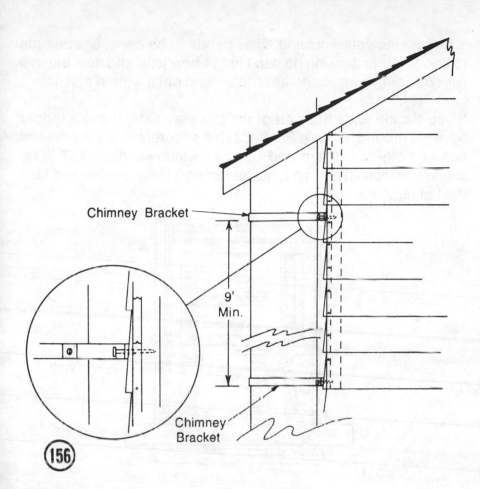

Chimney Bracket

9'
Min.

Chimney
Bracket

(156)

CAUTION—WORK SAFELY

Making an installation so it works perfectly requires following every step and especially the last one. This concerns installation of the flashing and housing and working on the roof. If you fear height or are subject to dizzy spells, don't even consider doing this part of the job. Talk to a roofer after you learn how the job should be done. Show the roofer all the illustrations concerning roof framing, flashing, chimney housing and slip section. Explain how each step is done so he knows you know. Tell him what you want done and note his reaction. If he's smart he won't resent your knowing exactly how the flashing, housing and a cricket is installed. And if he wants the job, he'll do the work at a fair price.

If he resents your knowing what needs to be done, or attempts to con you into thinking he can't judge how long and how much it will cost, get yourself another roofer, and get a written estimate.

If you decide to do this part of the job, play safe. Place a ladder on solid ground, or on a 2 x 8. Lash it securely to 2 x 4's placed across both downstairs and upstairs windows, Illus. 157. If no window is close by, run a taut line through two windows and lash the ladder to the line.

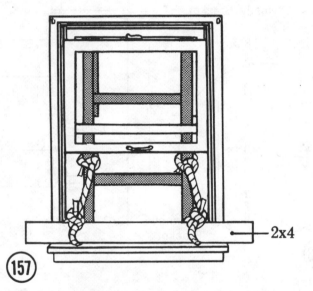

2x4

(157)

Working on a roof not only requires caution and guts, but also proper shoes. Playing safe indicates intelligence. Don't take chances. Wear ankle high, laced rubber-soled, non-skid keds, Illus. 158. Don't use slip-ons or low shoes. Wear as little loose clothing as weather permits. Only work on a roof when you have someone on the ground who can give you a hand when help is needed.

(158)

MAKE A ROOFER'S SAFETY HARNESS

Buy or make a body harness, Illus. 159, and a roofer's safety line, Illus. 160. When you lash a ladder in position, fasten a roofer's safety line to 2 x 4's across the inside of a first and second floor window, then put on a body harness and attach this to the safety line, you learn to walk and work on a roof as easily and as confidently as you can work in an attic.

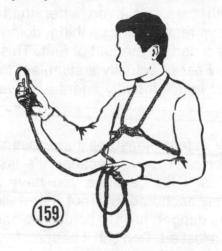

Whether you work on the roof or hire someone to do it, be sure to pull the plug on your TV, and to disconnect the antenna at the set. Ask your TV repair man whether your antenna holds an electrical charge.

Use caution when working on a roof. Never work near a power line or go up on the roof before, during or directly after a rainstorm, or when the morning dew makes it slippery, or on a windy day. Two other important No, No's. Don't go up on the roof when you are tired, or upset after an argument. Roof work requires a cool, clear mind.

Working on a roof after proper precautions have been taken isn't difficult, and with care, it's even safer than crossing many streets. But always remember one thing, doing anything for the first time creates a certain amount of fear. This is a normal and natural reaction. Fear is actually a stimulant that sharpens the senses. Consider fear a friendly agent who wants to keep you well and alive.

When necessary safety measures have been taken, and you realize the ladder can't move because it's lashed securely in place; and you can't fall because you have a body harness safety line securely anchored to a roof line, walking and working on a roof loses its danger, but still holds its glamor. Being a man is fast becoming a lost art. Don't let it happen to you.

The smart and safe way to work on a roof is to use a rope body harness, Illus. 159, and roof safety line, Illus. 160. The body harness is available readymade at boat supply stores, or through mail order, or you can easily make one using ⅜" nylon line. Nylon has a breaking strength of 3400 lbs.

For the roof safety line, use ⅜" nylon. To protect the line and the shingles on ridge, slide line through a two foot or longer length of 1" or ¾" discarded garden hose. To do this, straighten out a wire coat hanger. Make a half inch bend at one end. Tie a 3 or 4' length of twine to bend, then press bend together with pliers. Tie other end of twine to ⅜" nylon. Insert and pull wire, twine and rope through hose, Illus. 160.

Use sufficient length of nylon so you can make 3" loops every 3' on the side of roof you are working on, and still be able to work around chimney.

Tie a long free end of a ball of kite cord to a rubber ball. Tie the other end to the nylon roof line. Toss the ball and kite line over ridge. Draw nylon over ridge and tie this end to a 2 x 4 x 6' placed across top half of a second floor window. Position line where needed and anchor other end to another 2 x 4 across a window on a first floor.

When you get up on roof, slide hose over ridge. Have someone take up slack in roofer's line fastened to 2 x 4 across first floor window after you have achieved working position. Be sure to tell everyone in the house what you plan on doing so no lunkhead backs a car into the ladder, or removes same while you are on the roof. And under no circumstances anchor a safety line to a car unless you remove and hide the wheels.

Wearing clothes you will be wearing while working on roof, measure your chest girth, multiply by two and add 10". Cut a ⅜" line to length required, Illus. 161.

4" from each end, wrap line with nylon thread, separate, and tape ends of three strands, then splice ends together, Illus. 162.

Splice another line to make a 15" neck halter, Illus. 163. If you can't splice, tie a knot.

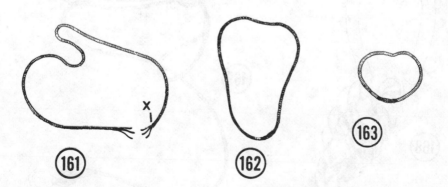

Place body loop through neck loop, Illus. 164; place in position shown, Illus. 165; wrap with nylon thread at G, also at H, Illus. 166.

Cut a safety line, 6 or 8'. Make 4" eyes at ends, Illus. 167.

Fasten a snap safety hook to one end, Illus. 168. Slip line through hoops, Illus. 169. Use this as your body safety line. Always hook body safety line to loops in roofing line.

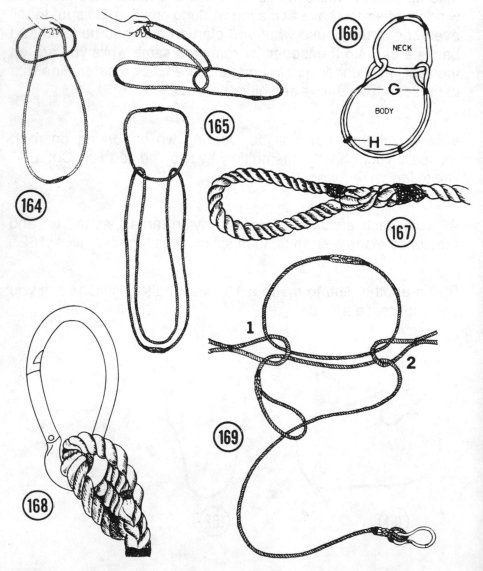

TO BUILD A CHIMNEY CRICKET

While a heavy snow seldom creates problems for an 18 x 18" single flue housing, the 38" side of a double housing, installed parallel to ridge on a steep roof, Illus. 170, creates a pocket. If you have a choice, position the 18" width parallel to ridge.

In areas where heavy snows are common, build a cricket. This is built and flashed after housing has been installed.

In Illus. 170, when roof pitch is 12" in 12" and Y measures 38", X should be 19". When ½" exterior plywood or wood sheathing is nailed to form a roof, overall height will measure 20" plus.

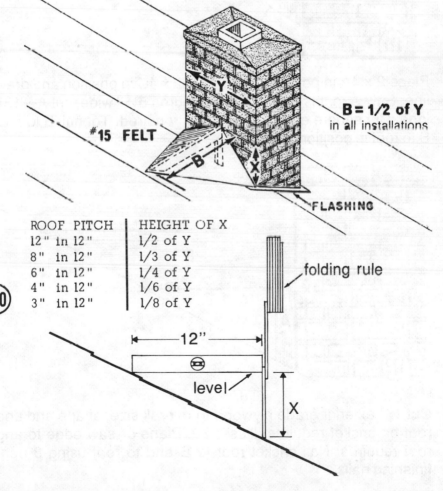

B = 1/2 of Y
in all installations

#15 FELT

FLASHING

ROOF PITCH	HEIGHT OF X
12" in 12"	1/2 of Y
8" in 12"	1/3 of Y
6" in 12"	1/4 of Y
4" in 12"	1/6 of Y
3" in 12"	1/8 of Y

(170)

folding rule

12"

level

X

Level 2 x 6B above actual position required, Illus. 171. Place 2 x 6D on roof and draw a line to indicate top edge of D. Saw end of B to this line.

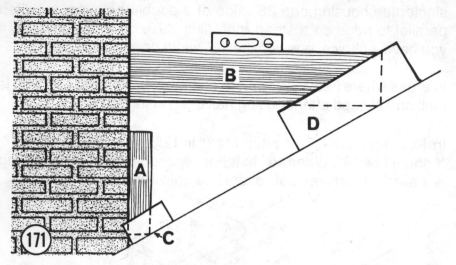

Place 2 x 4A in position, Illus. 171; 2 x 4C in position and draw a line. Saw A to this angle. If B measures 5½" wide, cut A—13½" long. Cut square end of B to length required. Toenail B to A and B to roof in position shown, Illus. 172.

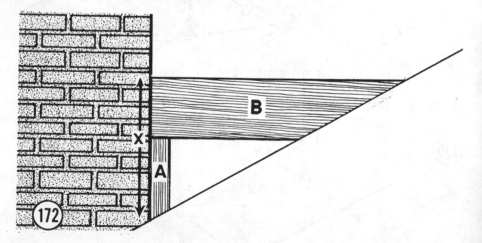

Cut ½" exterior grade plywood to overall size, shape and angle roof on cricket requires, Illus. 170. Plane or saw edge to angle roof requires. Nail cricket roof to B and to roof using 8 penny finishing nails.

114

Cover cricket with aluminum flashing. Cut flashing to shape required, Illus. 173, so at least 2" can be inserted under shingles on both sides of cricket, and the 1" lip can be bonded with epoxy and fastened with sheet metal screws to chimney housing.

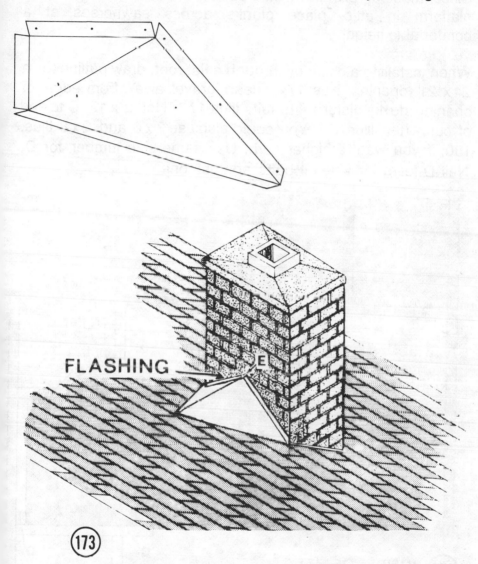

FLASHING

(173)

Raise shingles and embed edge of flashing in asphalt cement. Apply cement to top of flashing before replacing shingles. Nail through shingles and outer edge of flashing. Cover all nailheads with asphalt cement.

CHIMNEY INSTALLATION
THROUGH A FLAT ROOF

Since most of this work can be done working off a raised platform in attic, place planks across sawhorses at a comfortable height.

When installing a chimney through a flat roof, draw outline for a 21 x 21" opening, Illus. 174* Clean gravel away from edge of opening, do not disturb #15 felt, Illus. 176. Nail 2 x 12 C to end of cut rafter, Illus. 175. You could also use 2 x 6 and 2 x 8 Illus. 180, if you want a higher curb. Use same size lumber for D, Nail D to rafter when it butts against one.

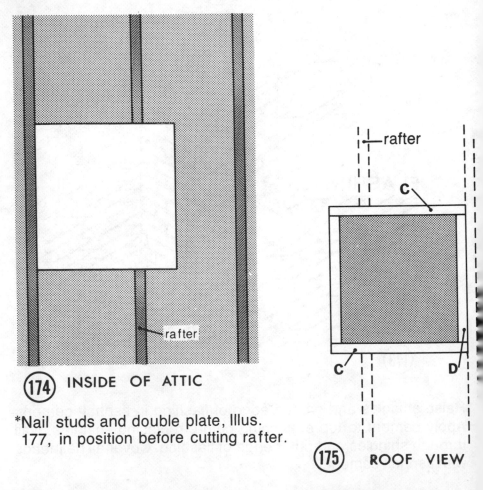

(174) INSIDE OF ATTIC

(175) ROOF VIEW

*Nail studs and double plate, Illus. 177, in position before cutting rafter.

Cut 2 x 6 to width required for E, Illus. 176. Note how joints overlap. Nail E with three 16 penny nails at each corner. Nail inner frame to outer one.

Nail a 1½ x 1½ x 1½" cant strip, G, Illus. 177, in position.

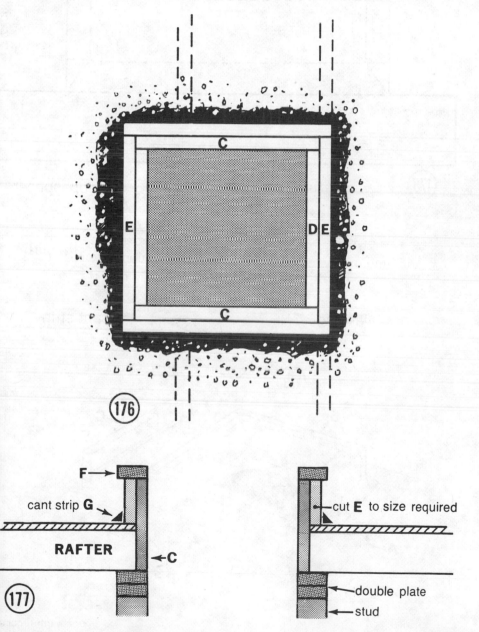

Cut and bend four 12" wide strips of flashing,* Illus. 178, to length curb requires. Solid line indicates cut lines; dash line indicates where flashing is bent. Using the curb as a form, bend flashing to shape shown, Illus. 179.

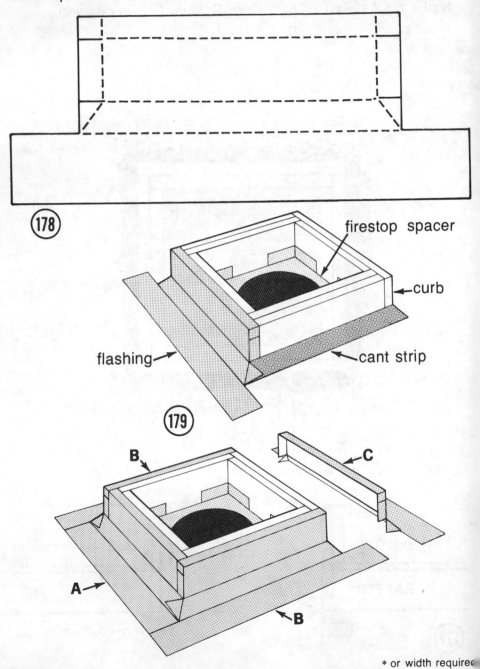

(178)

firestop spacer

curb

flashing

cant strip

(179)

B

C

A

B

* or width required

Position A then B and C.

Remove flashing and apply a 4 to 5" wide ribbon of asphalt cement around edge of opening.

Making certain ends of flashing overlap in position indicated, Illus. 179, bend flashing over top edge of curb, Illus. 180. Nail flashing to top of E using 1" aluminum nails with aluminum flashing. Space nails about 12" apart. Nail A then B and C flashing to curb. You can either solder overlapping corners or bond corners with epoxy. Apply asphalt cement to flashing on roof. Spread gravel.

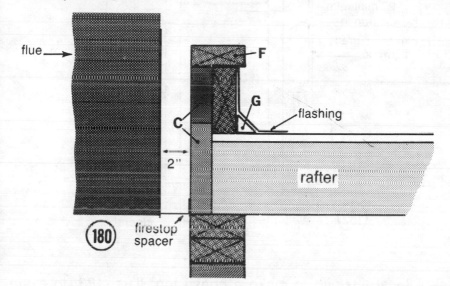

flue

F

G

flashing

C

2"

rafter

(180) firestop spacer

Nail 2 x 4 shoe in position shown to top of curb, Illus. 181, using 16 penny nails.

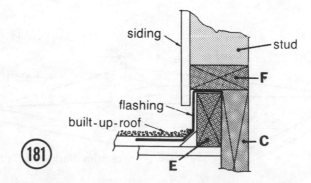

siding

stud

F

flashing

built-up-roof

C

(181)

E

Cut and nail studs and double plate, Illus. 182, in position to height required. Nail ⅜ or ½" exterior grade plywood to framing. Use ⅜" panels on a low housing, ½" on a taller one.

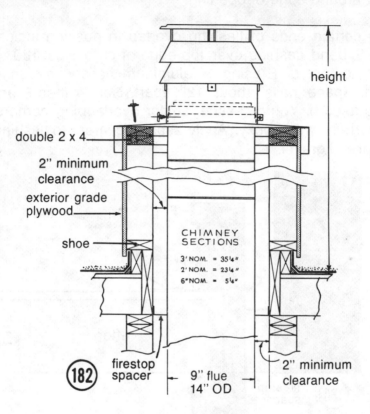

height

double 2 x 4

2" minimum clearance

exterior grade plywood

shoe

CHIMNEY SECTIONS

3' NOM. = 35¼"
2' NOM. = 23¼"
6" NOM. = 5¼"

(182) firestop spacer

9" flue 14" OD

2" minimum clearance

Ask a local tinsmith to make a chase top, Illus. 183, to exact dimension housing requires. Side flange on top should be 2" minimum. Collar at center should be not less than 2" high.

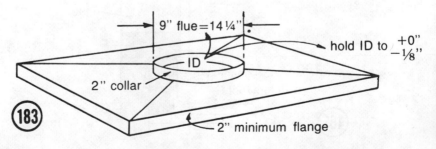

9" flue = 14¼"

hold ID to $^{+0"}_{-⅛"}$

ID

2" collar

(183)

2" minimum flange

Since the outside diameter of a 9" flue chimney may measure 14¼", ask your tinsmith to make a really tight fit. The 2" collar on top permits fastening a terminal cap, Illus. 184, supplied by manufacturer, to top of chimney. Note: Manufacturer also provides a cover with the terminal cap. This is installed in position shown following directions manufacturer packs with each accessory.

(184) Cap with Cover

Use sufficient number of 6", 2' and 3' sections to extend chimney to height above roof codes require. The chimney should project through a flat roof, 3' or more, Illus. 185.

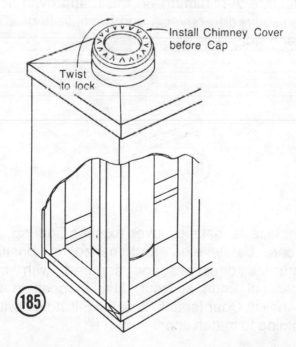

Install Chimney Cover
before Cap

Twist
to lock

(185)

Fasten chase top in position to housing with screws or nails.

Fasten terminal cap to chase top with locking collar bolt, Illus. 186. Manufacturer also recommends securing terminal cap with two 1" screws supplied. Follow directions manufacturer provides when installing a terminal cap.

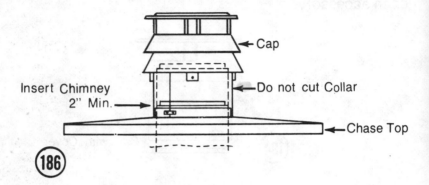

Cap

Insert Chimney
2" Min.

Do not cut Collar

Chase Top

(186)

INSTALLING A HEARTH

After walls adjacent to fireplace have been paneled or covered with gypsum board, install a prefabricated hearth, Illus. 187; ¾" or thicker slate. A minimum ⅜" thick, approved noncombustible hearth is required to cover a combustible floor 20" in front and 12" on each side, Illus. 34.

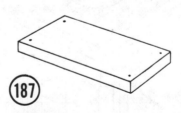

(187)

If the fireplace is installed over existing flooring, Illus. 188, the hearth can be leveled and nailed in position following manufacturer's directions, or secured with molding, Illus. 189. Miter cut ends at front. Nail in position with 6 penny finishing nails. Countersink heads. Fill holes with wood filler. Stain molding to match floor.

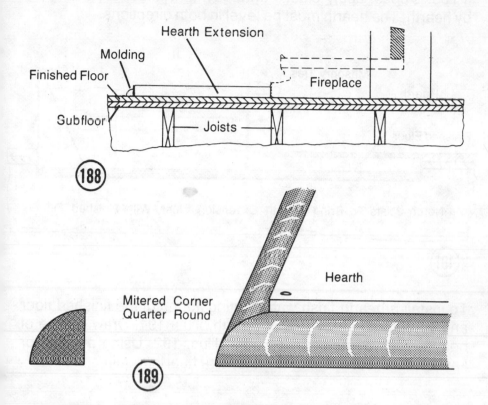

Hearth Extension

Molding

Finished Floor

Subfloor

Fireplace

Joists

(188)

Mitered Corner
Quarter Round

Hearth

(189)

A hearth extension can be placed over finished floor and can butt up against a raised fireplace, Illus. 190. Check floor with level. If level, place hearth in position, and again check with level in two directions.

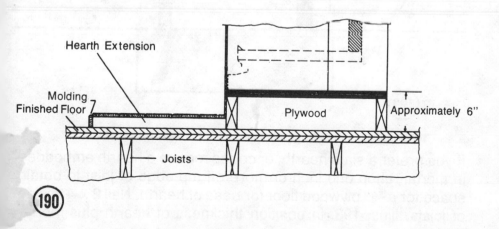

Hearth Extension

Molding
Finished Floor

Plywood

Approximately 6"

Joists

(190)

123

If floor slopes, apply plastic underlayment under area covered by hearth. The hearth must be level in both directions.

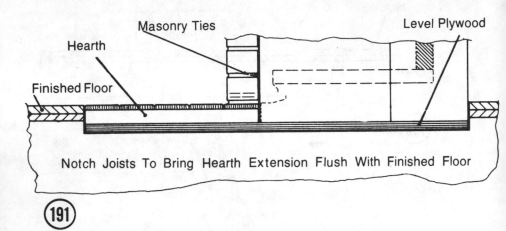

Notch Joists To Bring Hearth Extension Flush With Finished Floor

(191)

To install a hearth flush with existing floor, cut the finished floor and subfloor to exact size of hearth, Illus. 191. Draw outline of hearth. Drill ½" holes in corners, Illus. 192. Using a saber or keyhole saw, cut opening to exact size hearth requires.

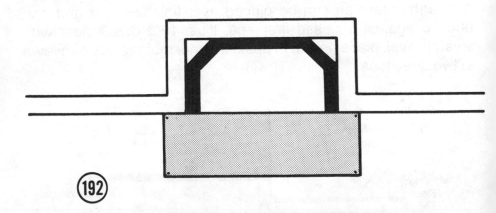

(192)

If you prefer a slate hearth, or codes require a hearth embedded in mortar, chop one inch or more off top edge of joist to obtain space for a ⅝" plywood floor for base of hearth. Nail 2 x 4 to side of joists, Illus. 193, in position thickness of hearth plus mortar

124

bed requires. Use a level to make certain 2 x 4's are level and an equal distance from finished floor. Mix one part cement, one half part lime to six parts sand. Spread at least 1" thick. The mortar bed must be level and at height that allows a slate or flagstone hearth to finish flush with finished floor, or height above desired. Test height of bed all around opening with a piece of wood equal in thickness to hearth. When bed checks out level and at height required, position slate and check it with level in two directions. Allow hearth to set at least 3 days before putting any weight on.

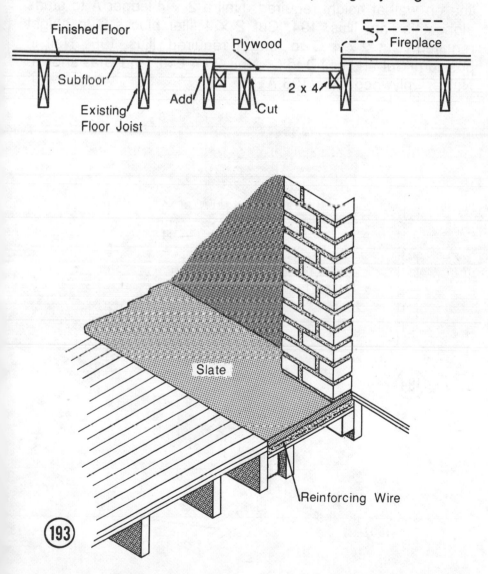

TO BUILD A RAISED PLATFORM

Decide what height you want. If you want to face the fireplace with brick, or with tile, Illus. 36, check size of brick and build platform to height that eliminates any need to cut the tile or brick, Illus. 66. Four courses of 2¼" brick, laid with a ⅜" mortar joist will measure 10½".

After deciding height of finished platform, use a 4' level to draw a line on wall at height required. Nail a 2 x 4 ledger A to studs along this line, Illus. 194. Cut 2 x 4 filler blocks B to height required. Cut 2 x 4 C to length required, Illus. 195. Nail in position. Cut and nail D to C Nail 2 x 4 E, F and G as shown. Nail ⅝" plywood, Illus. 196 A.

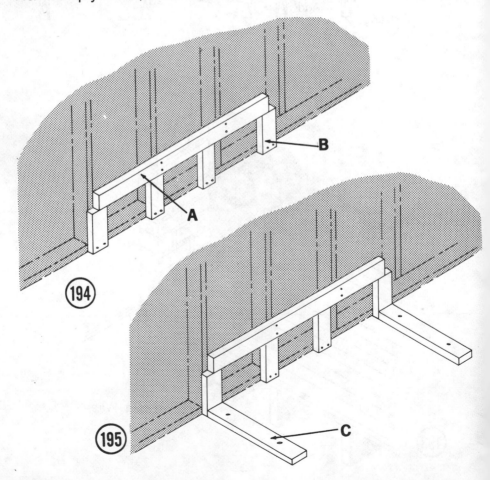

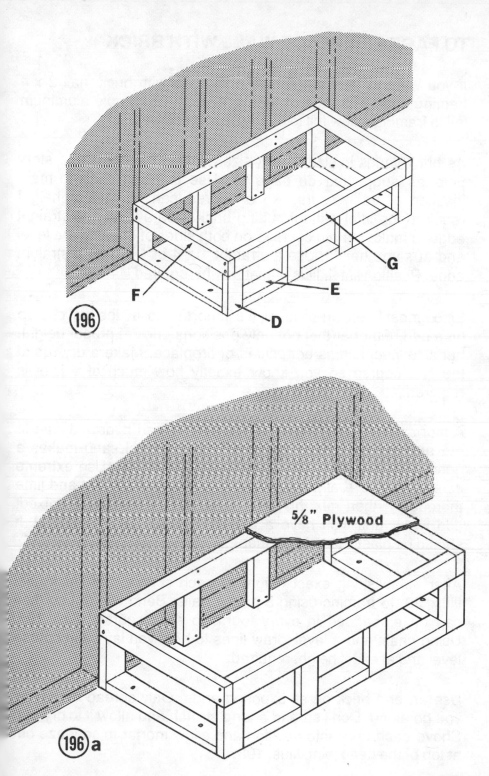

196

F D E G

196a

5⁄8" Plywood

TO FACE FIREPLACE WALL WITH BRICK

If you want to face a fireplace enclosure with brick, nail 2 x 4 framing flush with face of fireplace, Illus. 35. Staple aluminum foil to framing, allow foil to overlap each course 2".

As brick varies in size, check size available then make a story pole as suggested on page 53. Use this and chalk to mark location of each course so a course can be laid at height required for lintel without cutting brick. Use a level and straight edge to make certain courses on both sides of opening are level and at same height. Use a straight 1 x 4 or 1 x 6 as a straight edge. Position lintel, Illus. 44, at height required.

Since most floors aren't level, it's important to lay the first course on a bed of mortar that not only positions brick at proper height, but also level across both sides of fireplace. Make a dry run of the first course so you know exactly how much of a joint is required.

A mortar mix containing 1 part cement, 1 part hydrated lime to 4½ and not more than 6 shovels of screened sand makes a good brick mortar; or buy a prepared mortar mix. Use extreme care to measure all parts accurately. Mix the cement and lime thoroughly, then mix this with sand. When thoroughly mixed, add water until you have a plastic mixture. Test a handful. It should be plastic to hold its shape.

After establishing exact height of each course, nail brick ties, Illus. 39, to framing using 8 penny nails. Bend ties out so they can be embedded in every fourth to sixth course, Illus. 197. Using chalk and a level, draw lines to help you lay each course level and at exact height required.

Use an end brick on all exposed ends. Only spread mortar as you go along. Don't spread a long stretch and allow it to dry out. Shove each brick into position and allow mortar to squeeze out at top of the head joint, Illus. 198.

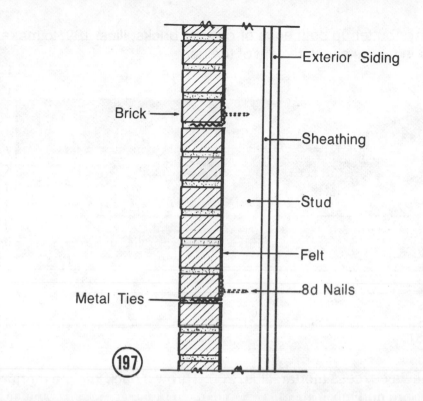

Brick →

Exterior Siding

Sheathing

Stud

Felt

8d Nails

Metal Ties

(197)

(198)

129

Always butter up both ends of closure bricks, Illus. 199, to make certain mortar squeezes out of the bed.

level guide line

Cut away excess mortar, Illus. 200. Throw it back into the mortar on board and mix it in.

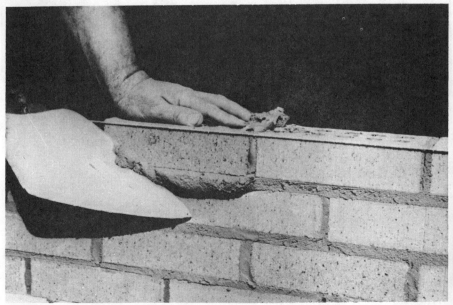

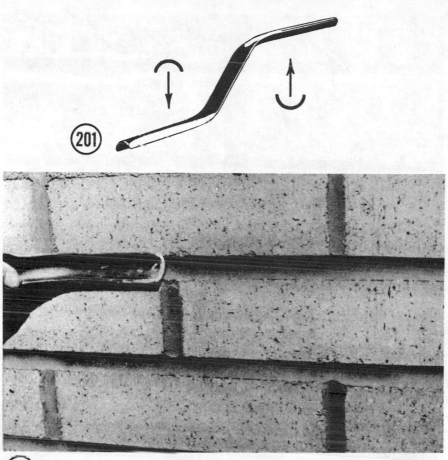

Concave Jointer

Use a concave jointer, Illus. 201, if you want a concave joint, Illus. 202; a V jointer, Illus. 203, if you want a V joint, Illus. 204. Use the jointer after laying up two or three courses. This gives mortar a chance to hold its shape.

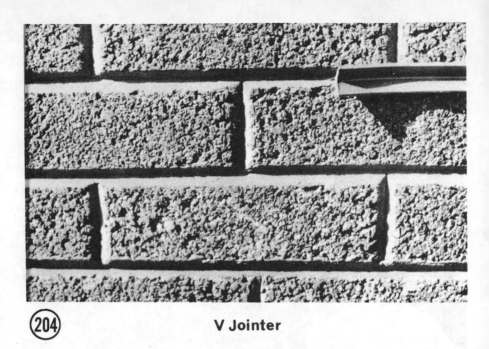

V Jointer

Illus. 205 shows various mortar joints you can use. A troweled joint (3, 4, 5) is one where the mortar is cut off with the trowel and finished with the trowel.

Mortar Joints

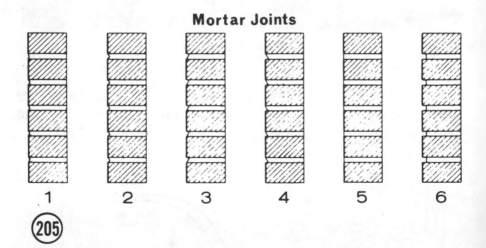

(205)

The weathered joint, Illus. 205-3, must be worked from below course using a trowel. Use a piece of ⅜" plywood to recess joint, Illus. 205-6.

132

Bend the brick ties into every fourth or sixth course. These can be spaced every 16" to 24" both horizontally and vertically. Book #668 Bricklaying Simplified provides much helpful information on the subject.

MASONRY FIREPLACE AND CHIMNEY

When you have selected a suitable location and have decided size of fireplace you want to build, snap chalk lines on floor to indicate width of fireplace. Draw plumb lines on wall to outline opening in wall. If part, or all of the chimney is to be constructed outside, draw a center line to indicate center of chimney. Draw lines equal distance from center to indicate overall width.

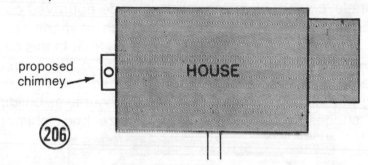

proposed chimney→

HOUSE

206

If fireplace is placed flush with the interior wall, the existing house foundation, Illus. 206, provides 8 or 10" of support. Measure from inside face of basement wall when laying out foundation for a chimney. Excavate area to depth below frost level required. After pouring foundation to within 6 to 8" from grade, place a 2 x 6 (5½") or 2 x 8 (7¼") form in position, Illus. 207. Position form on globs of concrete. Make certain it's level in two directions. Then complete pouring foundation as previously described.

FRONT VIEW

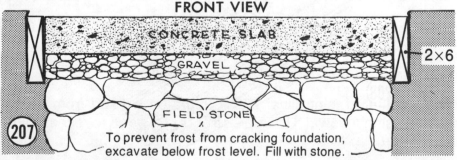

CONCRETE SLAB

GRAVEL

2×6

FIELD STONE

207

To prevent frost from cracking foundation, excavate below frost level. Fill with stone.

133

In new construction and in modernization work, a masonry fireplace and chimney foundation must go down below frost level, Illus. 60. If you dig a hole with straight sides, you won't need more than a 2 x 6 as a form just below grade level, You can use fieldstone and concrete to fill foundation.

The stone and concrete for a foundation must rest on undisturbed soil. Don't leave any loose dirt in excavation when you pour the foundation. Concrete for a foundation can be a 1-3-5 mix. This means 1 bag of cement (1 cubic foot) to 3 cubic feet of screened sand to 5 cubic feet of gravel. Buy readymix for a large foundation or rent a small concrete mixing machine.

While a single course of facing brick is code approved construction around a metal or refractory fireplace, in many areas a building inspector requires 8" of brick, Illus. 208. In this case lay two courses. Always lay brick so joints on adjoining courses are staggered in position shown. Always embed brick-to-brick reinforcing wire, Illus. 209, in every 2, 3 or 4th course as building inspector suggests. Build foundation to size brick chimney requires;

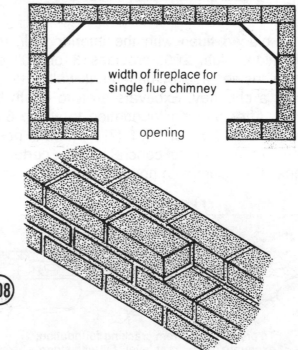

width of fireplace for single flue chimney

opening

(208)

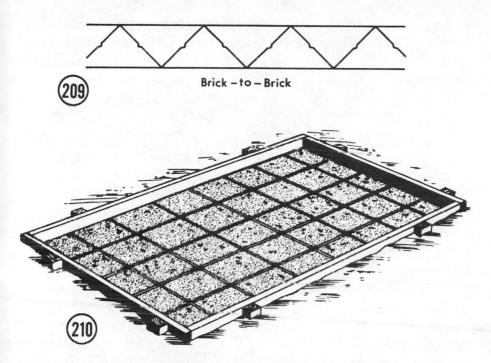

Brick – to – Brick

(209)

(210)

Most chimney builders lay the slab at,or just below grade level, Illus. 207. 1½ to 2" below top edge of foundation form, ombed 6 x 6 reinforcing wire, Illus. 210, then screed concrete level with form, Illus. 211, using a 2 x 4 across top of form. Work this back and forth. Allow slab to begin to set, then score it with a stick or screw driver, Illus. 212. Allow foundation to set three days before starting fireplace.

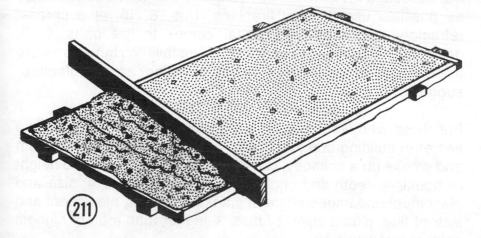

(211)

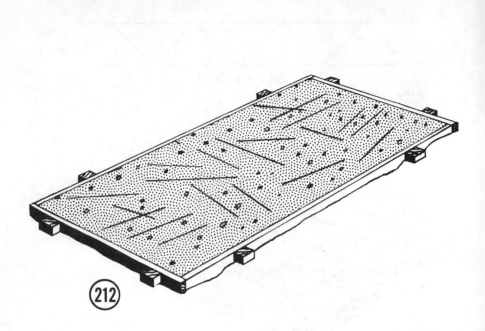

(212)

The chimney must be planned to contain a separate flue for each fireplace, another flue for the furnace. Never attempt to use one flue for a fireplace and furnace, or for two fireplaces. Illus. 213 indicates a three flue chimney. One serves the furnace, the other two provide flues for fireplaces.

To permit amateurs to build a masonry fireplace and chimney like a pro, and to insure constructing one that works as efficiently as possible use a metal fireplace, Illus. 6, 10, or a precast refractory firebox, Illus. 51, that comes in five parts. Both, designed by experts, not only simplify installation but also insure a satisfactory performance when installed as manufacturer suggests.

For those who want to build a firebrick firebox and hearth, the secret to building one that draws well, throws heat into a room and smoke up a chimney, is determined by the width and height of opening, depth and angle of back wall, Illus. 214; size and placement of damper, angle of smoke chamber, placement and size of flue, plus a chimney built 3' higher than roof, or highest point of roof within 10'.

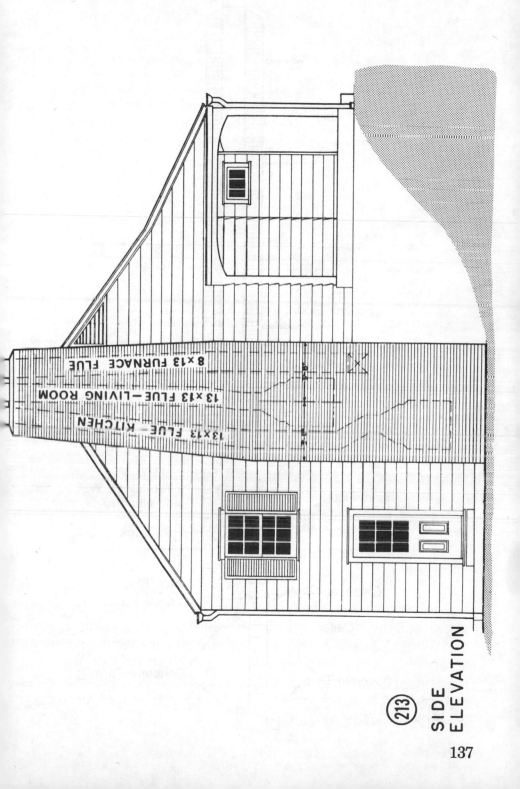

8×13 FURNACE FLUE

13×13 FLUE—LIVING ROOM

13×13 FLUE — KITCHEN

213 SIDE ELEVATION

137

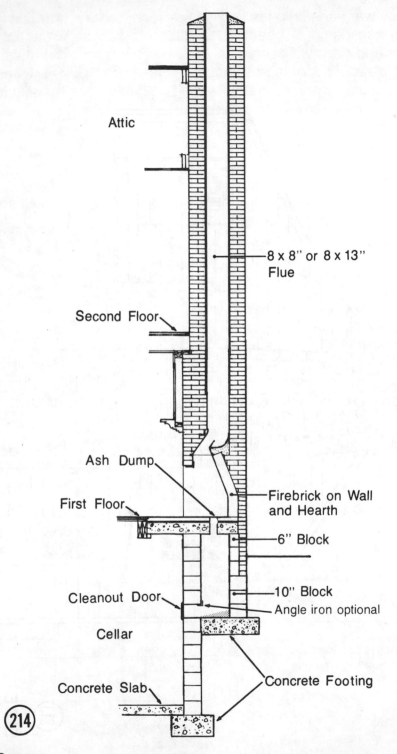

Attic

8 x 8" or 8 x 13" Flue

Second Floor

Ash Dump

Firebrick on Wall and Hearth

First Floor

6" Block

Cleanout Door

10" Block

Angle iron optional

Cellar

Concrete Slab

Concrete Footing

214

If you want an ash pit in floor of fireplace, order a refractory unit with ash dump in hearth, Illus. 51, or purchase an ash dump door and cleanout door, Illus. 215. Position same where shown. The cleanout door is positioned in base of chimney. Use flue tile as a chute or an aluminum heating duct can be used as a form. Place this in position so it connects to a cleanout door in base.

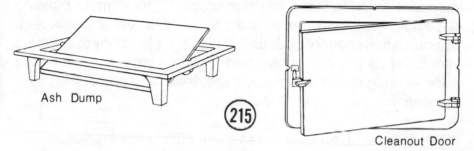

Ash Dump

(215)

Cleanout Door

When foundation reaches height of hearth, the floor joists are framed to allow for a hearth extension. This should be 20" deep and extend a minimum of 12" to each side of opening, Illus. 34. If you use a prefabricated hearth extension, Illus. 187, this doesn't require any mortar or special framing. It can be spiked in position over finished flooring. When building a masonry foundation, embed reinforcing rods, Illus. 216, so they can project into mortar bed for hearth extension.

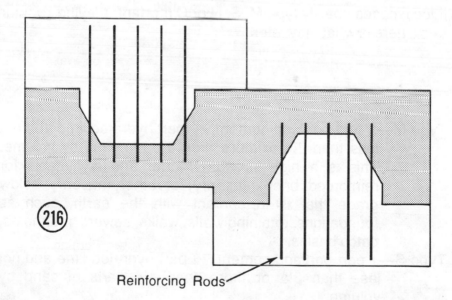

(216)

Reinforcing Rods

If you want the hearthstone to finish flush with finished floor, Illus. 193, lay sufficient concrete to bring foundation up to thickness of flagstone, plus 1" for mortar required. If you allow 1" for slate or flagstone, and 1" for mortar, build your hearth foundation to within 2" of finished floor. This construction provides a cantilevered foundation for your hearth. It is important to understand this construction since many building inspectors may question your ability to construct a fireplace. If you can answer every question, it's difficult for them to refuse a permit. Since you may easily find "building fireplaces" real nice work, and highly remunerative, read, learn and practice on your installation.

When foundation for hearth has been built to level required, and faced with brick, firebrick is laid within area required for fireplace. If you use a metal or prefabricated refractory unit, this contains a hearth for firebox.

As previously mentioned, firebrick for a hearth, side and back of a firebox is laid with fire clay, not cement mortar. Fire clay is available from your building supply dealer. Use exactly as directions specify.

If local codes specify type M, S, N or O mortar for laying regular brick, here is what they refer to.

Type M—1 part portland cement, ¼ part hydrated lime and not less than 2¼ or more than 3 parts sand by volume. This is a high strength mortar and is suitable for reinforced brick masonry, or other masonry below grade that is in contact with the earth, such as foundations, retaining walls, walks, sewers, manholes, catch basins.

Type S—1 part portland cement, ½ part hydrated lime and not less than 3½ or more than 4½ parts of sand by volume.

Type N—1 part portland cement, 1 part hydrated lime and not less than 4½ or more than 6 parts sand by volume. This mortar is considered a medium strength mortar and is recommended for exposed masonry above grade, walls, chimneys, and exterior brick work subject to severe exposure.

Type O—1 part portland cement, 2 parts hydrated lime and not less than 6¾ or more than 9 parts of sand. This mortar is suitable for non load-bearing walls.

The metal fireplaces, Illus. 6, 10, and the refractory firebox, Illus. 51, come with a hearth. All you add is the hearth extension, Illus. 34. This can be the prefabricated hearth, Illus. 187; or ¾" slate or flagstone.

Those wanting to lay up a firebrick hearth and firebox lining, as well as a brick chimney, should remember one simple fact. If you can lay one brick properly, you can lay a hundred. All it takes is time, a clear mind and labor. Bricklaying is a form of exercise that's far superior to golf in keeping the mind and muscle in condition. It offers physical as well as mental therapy that helps relieve tension. After reading through this book, and while still wondering whether you possess the skill, buy a few bricks, a bag of mortar mix, trowel, a chalk line and a level, then practice. Invest as much time as you would at a driving range or watching a sporting event on TV. Snap chalk lines on the floor of the garage, or place the fireplace template, Illus. 2, in position. Lay out a course of brick dry, no mortar, Illus. 207, around the template or fireplace unit selected. Use a piece of ⅜" plywood as a spacer guide. Space each brick ⅜" apart. Use the level as a straight edge. Next cover floor with a piece of polyethylene, and lay out each brick using mortar.

Bricklaying requires constant use of a level horizontally, vertically, as well as diagonally, Illus. 217. It requires constant use of a level guide line, Illus. 199. To make certain a guide line is level and at exact height each course requires, wrap the line around level end bricks placed on ⅜" mortar joint, Illus. 218, or use corner guides, Illus. 219. Check line with a line level.

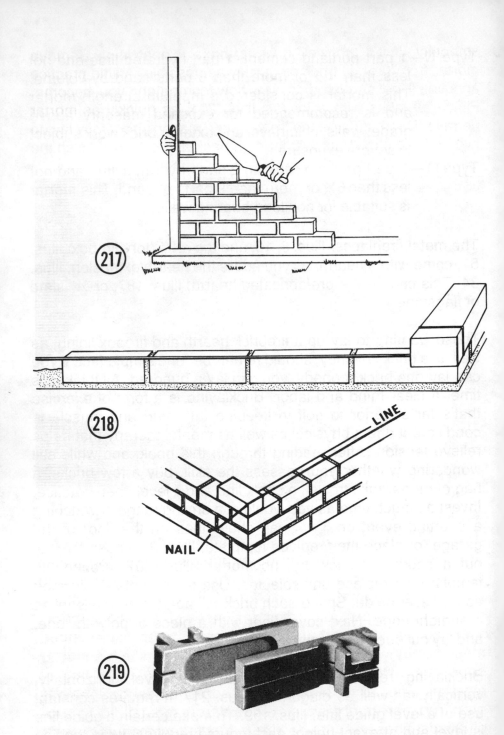

Brick mortar must be plastic. Moist, but not wet. Squeeze a handful. It should hold its shape. If it's too dry, it won't spread smoothly. If it's too wet, it won't make a neat joint. Remove mortar from face of brick as quickly as possible. A little practice and you'll be surprised to see how competent you become. Finish all joints with a jointer, Illus. 201, as quickly as mortar permits. Depending on the heat of day, masons generally lay up two or three short courses, then go back and carefully finish the joints.

220

If you decide to build a block foundation rather than pour one, use size blocks specified by local codes. Before laying blocks check guide lines to make certain they are square, level and taut. Check diagonals to make sure lines are square. Setting blocks takes some skill, common sense and a lot of practice. You can learn much by working alongside an experienced mason or by watching one work. Most masons use a mortar consisting of one bag of portland cement, 1/3 to 1/2 bag of mason's lime, 20 to 24 shovels of screened sand. Specially prepared mortar mixes are available from most building supply yards. These require no lime — just follow manufacturer's directions when mixing. Always keep your mortar alive by working it over, Illus. 220.

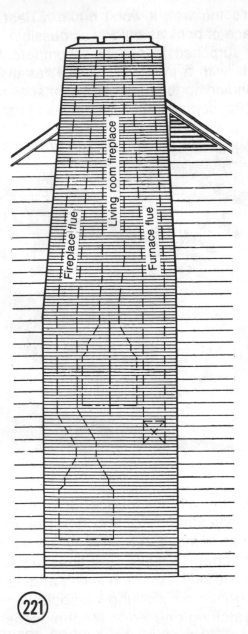

Fireplace flue

Living room fireplace

Furnace flue

(221)

If you plan on installing a fireplace in a basement playroom, another on a first or second floor, the same chimney can serve both units, Illus. 221, but each fireplace must have a separate flue. There are no exceptions. Flues in a chimney need not be the same size. Flue size is determined by fireplace opening.

144

Flues can be round, rectangular or square. Their shape and size determine overall size of chimney.

The story pole, Illus. 66, marked with thickness mortar joint and brick used, helps establish height of each course.

Lay brick, block or concrete to height of hearth. Illus. 222 shows a typical first course of brick for a two fireplace chimney. Illus. 223, shows the second course.

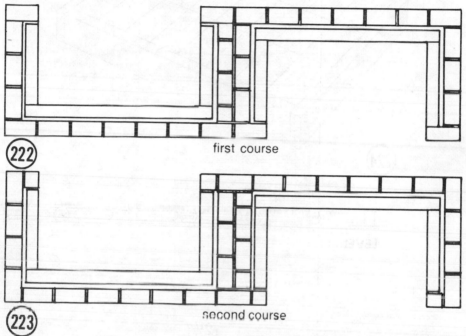

first course

second course

One of the easiest ways a beginner can get dry behind the ears learning to lay a level firebrick hearth to overall size hearth requires, is to make a 2 x 4 form to overall size of hearth. Check form with a carpenter's square, Illus. 224. Level form on globs of concrete at exact height required for hearth. Spread mortar within form to height required to lay each brick with fire clay joints level with form. Use an ⅛" joint on hearth. By checking brick with a level across form, you can lay the hearth quickly and easily.

Lay firebrick hearth to full width and depth needed. Hearth must provide a base for the sides and back of firebox.

145

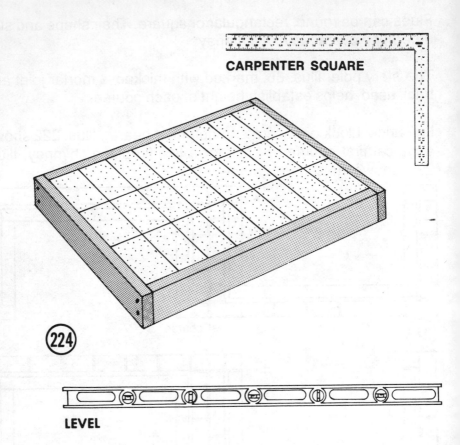

CARPENTER SQUARE

(224)

LEVEL

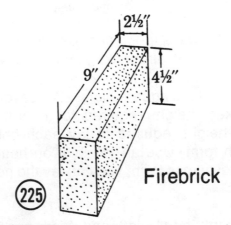

2½″

9″

4½″

Firebrick

(225)

(225)

Firebrick —4½" face exposed

Standard firebrick measures 9 x 2½ x 4½", Illus. 225. While the side and back of this fireplace, Illus. 226, was laid up with 2½" edge exposed, building codes now permit the hearth, sides and back laid with 4½" face exposed, Illus. 227. Use ⅛" joint when laying a hearth; ⅜" joint when laying up sides and back. 35 lbs. of fire clay will lay up approximately 100 firebrick with a minimum size joint.

The 36" wide by 29" opening in this all masonry fireplace, Illus. 226, was laid up with 2½" edge of firebrick placed in position shown.

Illus. 228 shows firebrick with the 4½" face lining firebox. This is code approved in many areas and offers considerable savings. Note position of lintel across opening, also the angle iron positioned two brick courses below flue, Illus. 226, 227.

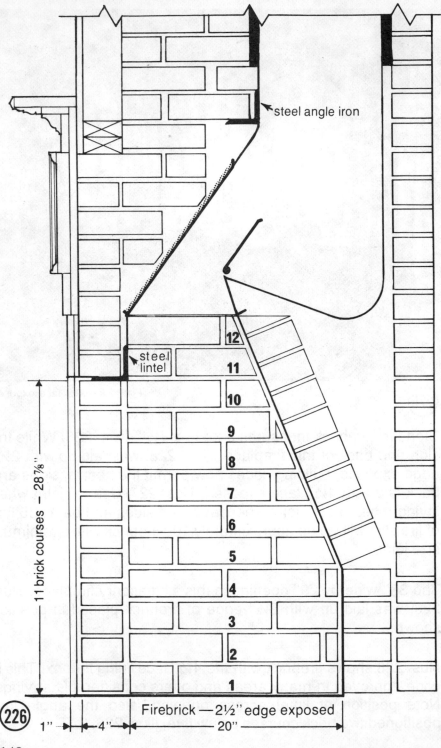

steel angle iron

steel
lintel

12
11
10
9
8
7
6
5
4
3
2
1

11 brick courses — 28⅞"

226

1" 4" Firebrick — 2½" edge exposed
              20"

148

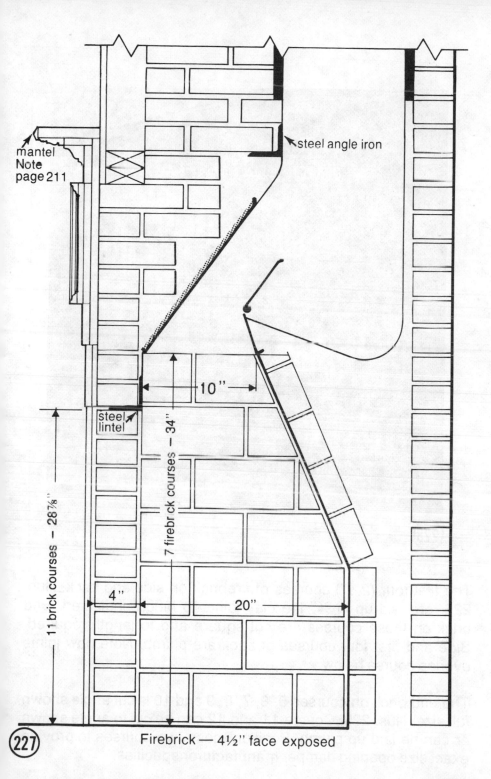

mantel
Note
page 211

steel angle iron

10"

steel
lintel

7 firebrck courses — 34"

11 brick courses — 28⅞"

4"

20"

227

Firebrick — 4½" face exposed

The first four (2½") courses of firebrick on side and back, Illus. 226, are laid up in ⅜" fire clay joints to height indicated. End brick on these courses are cut square and to length required. Side and first four courses of back are plumb. Note how joints overlap course below.

The end brick on courses 5, 6, 7, 8, 9 and 10 is cut angle shown full size, Illus. 229. Course 11 and 12 can be cut to angle shown or can be laid up plumb. Position these two courses to provide exact size opening damper manufacturer specifies.

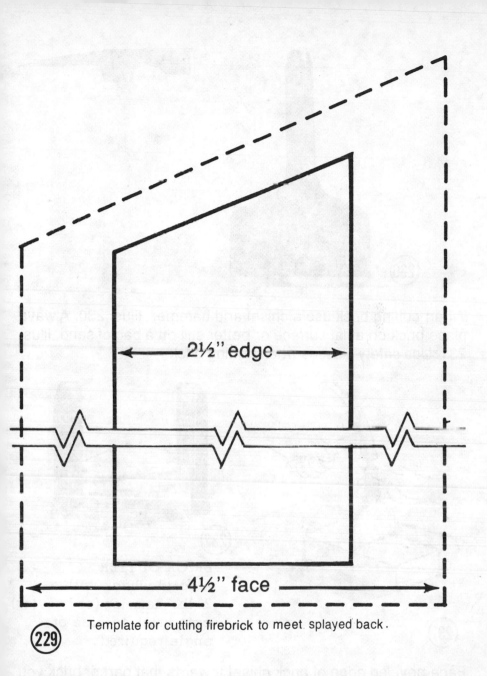

2½" edge

4½" face

Template for cutting firebrick to meet splayed back.

If you lay firebrick with 2½" edge exposed, using a ⅜" fire clay mortar joint, 10 courses will equal approximately 29"; 6 courses, if 4½" face is exposed. Any slight variation in overall height due to thickness of mortar joint will not affect the operation of a fireplace.

151

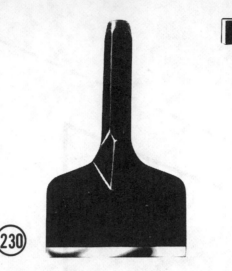

(230)

When cutting brick use a chisel and hammer, Illus. 230. Always place brick on a flat surface or better still on a bag of sand, Illus. 231. Use safety glasses when cutting brick.

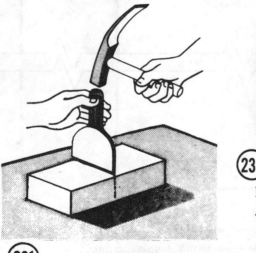

(231)

(232)

BRICK CUTTER
A solid whack with a 2-lb. hammer (or heavier) cuts brick to size or angle required.

Face beveled edge of brick chisel towards that part of brick you don't need. Many tool rental stores rent brick cutters, Illus. 232. These are great time, labor and brick saving devices.

Draw line on brick and place in cutter. Hit top of blade with a 2 lb. or heavier hammer and it makes a perfect cut.

Since some brick cuts easier than others, always ask a masonry supply retailer how he suggests cutting the brick you buy. Some will cut what you need for a small fee.

Fill in back of each course with concrete as you lay up each course of the firebox. Be sure to overlap joints as indicated, Illus. 226.

Trowel face all joints, Illus. 205-5. This means cutting fire clay off flush with face of brick.

To corbel ceiling of firebox to angle required, lay the 5th (2½" edge) side course with end bricks cut to angle of pattern, Illus. 229. Lay this course on back wall in a heavy bed of fire clay shaped as shown, Illus. 226, 227. Maintain the ⅜" joint on face of firebox. If you embed chips of brick when building this course, it stiffens joint and provides additional support needed to continue laying up firebox.

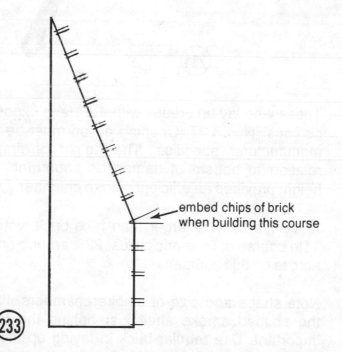

embed chips of brick
when building this course

(233)

To make certain all courses from the 5th up are laid to exact angle required, make a tester, Illus. 233. Cut 1 x 10* to angle and
* 1 x 10 or ⅜" plywood.

153

size shown. Locate and mark exact location of each course. Use a level to make certain all courses are level and sides are plumb.

When you reach the 10th course, (2½" edge exposed) overall height will be approximately 29". Lay two additional courses to provide opening at top flue manufacturer specifies. Embed the damper, Illus. 234, in position shown in a bed of brick mortar.

(234)

Those who lay up firebox with 4½" face exposed can lay seven courses, Illus. 227. Opening at top must be full width damper manufacturer specifies. The height of fireplace opening in relation to bottom of damper is important. The difference in height provides an efficient smoke chamber.

Since fire brick is larger than face brick, you will be laying the 11th course of face brick, Illus. 226, around opening. Place lintel across on this course.

Note shape and size of smoke chambers, Illus. 226. This and the shaped smoke shelf just behind the top of damper are important. Use regular brick in laying up the smoke chamber. Line smoke chamber with fire clay or brick mortar. Smoke chamber must be smooth and shaped as shown.

Set damper over opening in a bed of mortar. Check damper to make certain it's level in two directions. Remove all excess mortar around joint. Cover hood and ends of damper with rock wool insulation, Illus. 226, following manufacturer's directions. This allows metal casing to expand and contract without cracking masonry.

Use size flue tile manufacturer of damper specifies. Illus. 235, indicates flue size recommended by damper manufacturer.

A	Approx. B	C	D	E	F	G	H	Flue O.D. Under 20'
6	6	24-27	16	24	11	10	13½	8½"x13"
6	6	24-27	16	29	16	10	13½	8½"x13"
6	6	27-30	20	35	22	10	13½	13"x13"
9	6	30-33	20	41	28	10	13½	13"x18"
12	9	33-36	23	47	34	10	13½	18"x18"
12	9	36-42	23	53	40	10	13½	18"x18"
15	9	36-42	26	59	46	10	13½	18"x18"
18	9	36-48	26	71	58	10	13½	18"x24"

SPECIFICATIONS (Dimensions in inches)

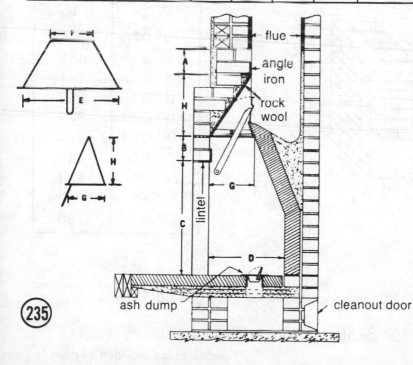

235

ash dump   cleanout door

flue
angle iron
rock wool
lintel

As previously mentioned, all mortar joints for flue tile must be smooth on inside and no mortar should be allowed to drop into damper. Continue laying up brick for chimney.

To prevent any droppings, stuff a burlap or other cloth bag tight with straw, hay, or old leaves. Tie a line to top of bag, keep pulling the bag up as you set each tile. The bag not only smoothes the joint but also prevents any mortar from dropping into damper.

Illus. 236 shows a brick layout for a chimney with a single 8½ x 8½" flue.

Illus. 237 indicates amount of brick required for various heights.

8 1/2" x 8 1/2"
Flue Lining

(236)

HEIGHT OF CHIMNEY	NUMBER OF BRICK ★
1' 0"	30
2' 0"	54
3' 0"	78
6' 0"	156
9' 0"	244
12' 0"	312
15' 0"	390
18' 0"	468
21' 0"	546
24' 0"	624
27' 0"	702
30' 0"	780

(237)

Illus. 238 shows a chimney with two 8½ x 8½" flues.

Illus. 239 indicates amount of brick this chimney requires.

156   *Specifications provided by manufacturer

2 - 8 1/2" x 8 1/2"
Flue Linings

HEIGHT OF CHIMNEY	NUMBER OF BRICK *
1' 0"	50
2' 0"	80
3' 0"	130
6' 0"	260
9' 0"	390
12' 0"	520
15' 0"	650
18' 0"	780
21' 0"	910
24' 0"	1040
27' 0"	1170
30' 0"	1300

Illus. 240 shows a chimney with one 8½ x 8½" and one 8½ x 13" flue.

Illus. 241 indicates number of brick required for a single course. Note: All quantities of brick were figured for a chimney with 4" of brick around flues.

1 ea. 8 1/2" x 8 1/2" & 8 1/2" x 13" Flue Lining

HEIGHT OF CHIMNEY	NUMBER OF BRICK *
1' 0"	55
2' 0"	99
3' 0"	143
6' 0"	286
9' 0"	429
12' 0"	572
15' 0"	715
18' 0"	858
21' 0"	1001
24' 0"	1144
27' 0"	1287
30' 0"	1430

157

You can build a chimney to any width and depth the flue tile and height above ridge requires. Look at other chimneys on houses similar to yours. Count the number of full and half brick to a course. Count bricks to ascertain overall width, also the depth.

If you need 8" of brick around a flue on exposed part of chimney, Illus. 242, it's O.K. to corbel bricks providing the angle does not exceed 1" per course, or more than 7" in one foot. Note how this chimney goes from a single 4" thick brick wall to 8" in four courses. Even in areas where codes approve 4" around flues, if chimney is likely to be subjected to high winds, or needs to be extended high above a roof, lay 8" of brick around exposed part of chimney.

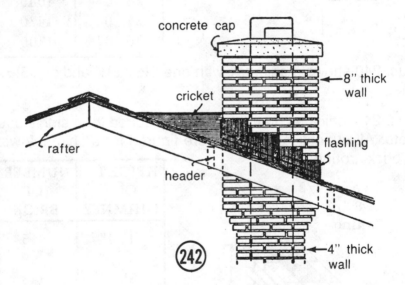

concrete cap

cricket

8" thick wall

rafter

flashing

header

(242)

4" thick wall

While the lower stages of a chimney can be handled working off planks across sawhorses, it's essential you build or rent a scaffold to simplify working in a comfortable manner. Since a scaffold needs to support you, a mortar board, mortar and bricks, it must be rigid. When built to height required it lessens fatigue by eliminating unnecessary bending and stooping. Don't rent or build a flimsy scaffold. Remember, it must provide solid support. Any movement in a scaffold is not only hazardous to you and anyone passing by, but also prevents laying brick accurately.

Illus. 243 shows a build-it-yourself scaffold that can be constructed to any height required. Use 2 x 4 or 2 x 6 for posts A. When you want to increase height, spike scabs, Illus. 244, to both sides of posts. Nail additional cross bracing B and D. Always use lumber free of knots for scaffolding.

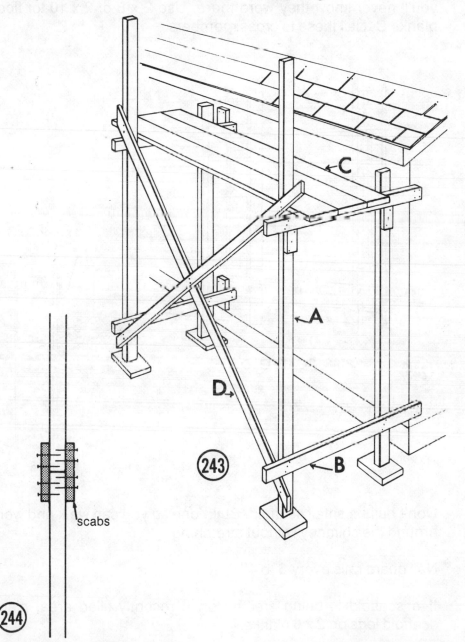

scabs

A good safety factor is to anchor scaffold to 2 x 4 blocks spiked to studs in wall, Illus. 245. Drive nails almost all the way. Just allow head of nail to project sufficiently to permit pulling with a wrecking bar. Don't worry about nail holes through siding. These can be filled with a wood filler, covered with a spot of paint and you'll never know they were there. Use 2 x 8 or 2 x 10 for floor planks C. Nail these to cross members.

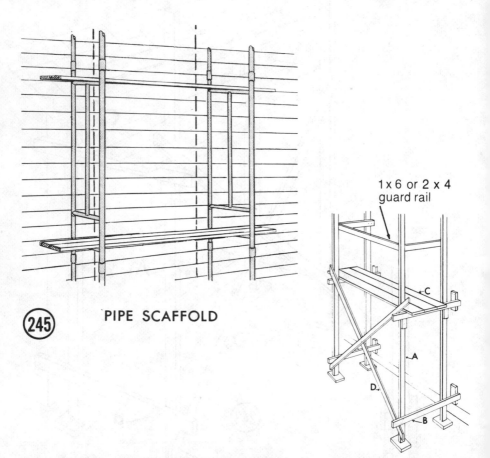

1 x 6 or 2 x 4
guard rail

(245) PIPE SCAFFOLD

Don't build a small scaffold. Build one so you can walk and work around the chimney without stretching.

Nail guard rails every 3 to 4' above C.

If a scaffold is being erected on a recently filled area, place scaffold legs on 2 x 6 planks.

160

BUILDING A CHIMNEY OUTSIDE HOUSE

When a metal fireplace unit is installed in a masonry chimney the manufacturer provides a fiber glass blanket. Cover unit with fiber glass following directions manufacturer provides. Don't crush insulation when building chimney. The insulation not only permits metal to retain heat, while it keeps heat away from masonry, but also allows metal to expand and contract without cracking masonry.

After drawing lines on outside of house to indicate overall width and shape of chimney, set an electric hand saw to cut through exterior siding only. Saw and remove siding within area to be covered by chimney. Reset saw and cut sheathing within area required for fireplace and that part of a chimney within house. Remove studs within area required for fireplace. Add jack studs at ends of opening, as noted, Illus. 246. Buy a piece of heavy gauge polyethylene to size required, to cover opening during construction. Staple this to a 1 x 2. Tack 1 x 2 above and down both sides of opening at night.

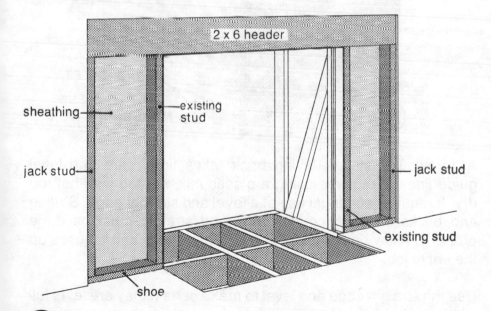

2 x 6 header

sheathing

existing stud

jack stud

jack stud

existing stud

shoe

246

Your building material or masonry supply dealer sells brick mortar mixes. These require sand and water. If you prefer to mix mortar, use 1 part cement, 1 part hydrated lime, 4½ to 6 parts of fine, screened sand.

Illus. 247 shows how to make a measuring tub that accommodates one bag of portland cement. A bag contains one cubic foot. By nailing ½" half round strips on inside, at 3, 6, and 9" from bottom, you can accurately measure amount of sand or cement in ¼, ½ or ¾ units.

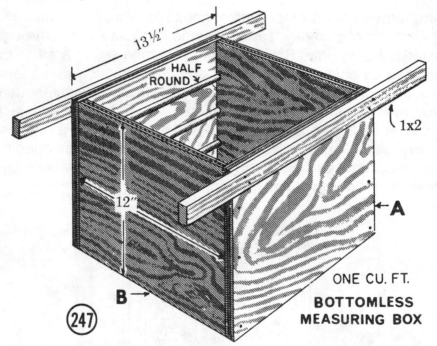

13½"

HALF ROUND

1x2

12"

A

B

ONE CU. FT.
BOTTOMLESS MEASURING BOX

(247)

As previously stated, laying brick takes time, care and level guide lines. It requires using a plastic mix, not too wet, not too dry. It requires continual use of a level and straight edge. Setting end bricks on each course level and straight must be done properly. Allow one course to be laid improperly and it louses up the entire job.

Use the straight edge and level to make certain they are level full width and depth of chimney. Make certain they are plumb vertically and diagonally.

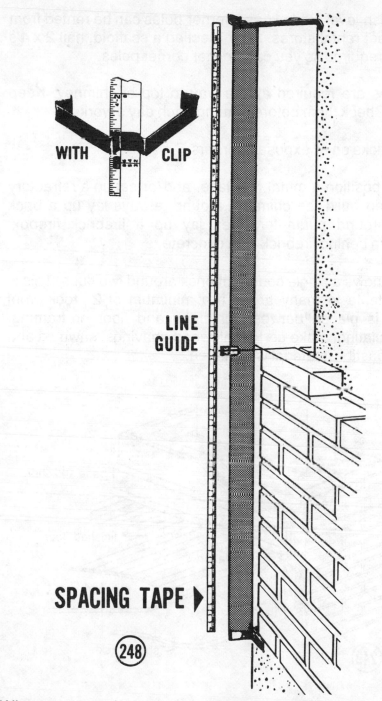

WITH CLIP

LINE GUIDE

SPACING TAPE ▶

(248)

When an experienced mason lays up a chimney, he sets up plumb corner poles, Illus. 248. These also provide level line clips that establish level guide lines. Corner poles can be rented from masonry tool rental stores. After erecting a scaffold, nail 2 x 4's in position required so you can anchor corner poles.

Plumb lines are required all the way to top of chimney. Keep lines taut. Check them before starting each day's work.

Use end bricks on all exposed corners.

While you position a metal fireplace, and/or set up a refractory firebox, then build the chimney around, always lay up a brick chimney around perimeter, then lay up a firebrick firebox. Always fill in behind firebrick with concrete.

Illus. 249 shows a single course of brick around two flues. This is still acceptable in many areas if a minimum of 2" rock wool insulation is placed between chimney and floor or framing. Before insulating, make certain all wood shavings, sawdust and other combustible material is removed.

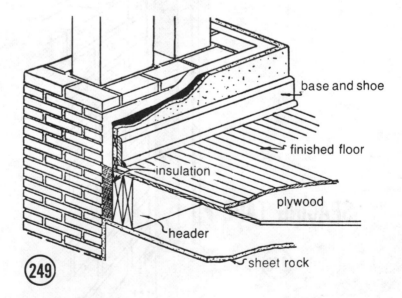

base and shoe

finished floor

insulation

plywood

header

sheet rock

(249)

Illus. 208 shows an 8" wall. Note that flues should be separated by 4" brick, Illus. 249.

The flue is a vitally important part of your fireplace. Select the proper size from chart shown, page 238. Don't deviate, don't improvise. This chart was developed from experience that proved the flue area should not be less than 1/12 of the area of the fireplace opening.

Cement flues end-to-end with cement mortar. If you find it necessary to corbel a flue, Illus. 250, cut a cardboard pattern to make certain you have the correct angle. Flues should be as straight as possible. If you need to corbel a flue, a 30° offset is permissable, Always use a full flue for an offset. While up to a 45° offset is frequently used, and permitted, it could create a problem under certain conditions.

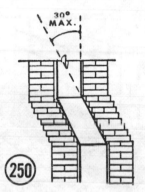

Cut flue using a table or electric hand saw with a carborundum blade, or use a chisel and hammer. Draw line of cut. Pack flue with sand before cutting with a brick chisel. If you have to cut several flues, use a bag of sand. Be sure sand fits tight in area being cut.

Mark line of cut with a pencil. Using a bricklayer's chisel and a hammer, Illus. 230, tap chisel lightly to score line ⅛" deep all around. Continue until flue is cut even depth and snaps. Smooth rough edges. Use sufficient mortar to make a tight, smooth joint.

Position flues a minimum of 4" apart. Stagger joints in adjoining flues to prevent any smoke escaping from one flue into another. Corbel flues with as little slope as possible.

165

INSTALLATION OF CHIMNEY THROUGH ROOF

Since a masonry chimney must be built on a separate foundation, and is thus subjected to settling that doesn't match that of house, it's important to flash it properly. Roofers generally follow this procedure when applying roofing and flashing around a chimney. After applying #15 felt to entire roof, they apply shingles up to bottom edge of chimney, Illus. 251.

Copper or zinc base flashing is cut to size and shape shown, Illus. 252. The top edge is bent over ½", Illus. 253. The bottom is embedded in asphalt cement and nailed in place over asphalt shingles. Embed lip in mortar, Illus. 254.

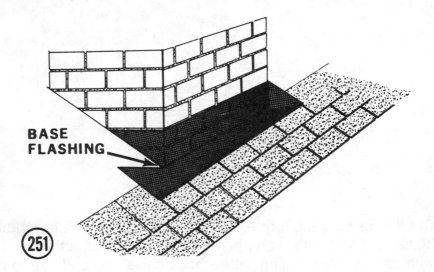

BASE FLASHING

(251)

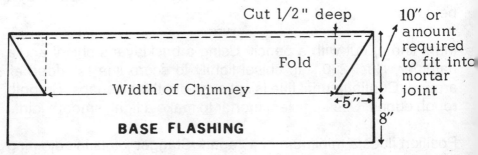

Cut 1/2" deep

Fold

Width of Chimney

←5"→

8"

10" or amount required to fit into mortar joint

BASE FLASHING

(252)

166

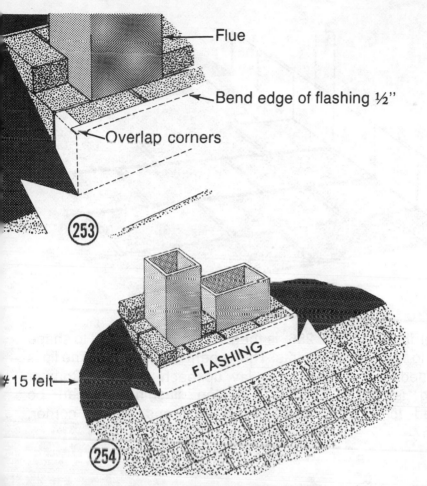

Flue

Bend edge of flashing ½"

Overlap corners

(253)

#15 felt →

FLASHING

(254)

Step flashing, Illus. 255, is cut to size indicated and nailed in position while applying each course of shingle up side of chimney.

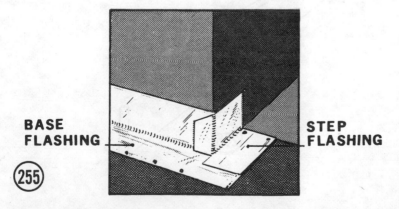

BASE
FLASHING

STEP
FLASHING

(255)

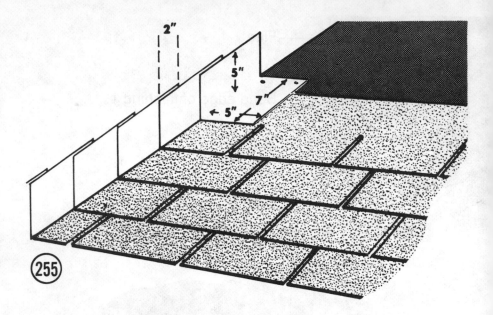

Counter flashing, Illus. 256, is then cut to size and bent to shape shown to fit into mortar joints. This is bent with a ½" lip. The lip is embedded in mortar as you lay up each course. Counter flashing is never bonded to step flashing. It can be soldered to base flashing where it wraps around corner, Illus. 257.

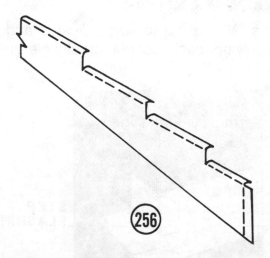

— solder this joint

(257)

Cut counter flashing so it projects well over edge of metal covering roof of cricket. Before applying counter flashing, seal point E with asphalt cement. Embed lip on counter flashing in mortar joints. Bottom edge overlaps and can be embedded in non-hardening cement to metal on roof of cricket, Illus. 173.

Build a chimney cricket following directions on page 113. Cover cricket roof with metal as shown, Illus. 173. Metal should extend beyond base of cricket so at least 2" can be covered by adjacent roofing shingles. Embed edge of metal in asphalt cement, then nail along extreme outside edge. Apply asphalt cement to fasten edge of shingle.

Install flue up as you build chimney to a point 24" above ridge of roof. Allow flue to project above cap, Illus. 258. Place a form in position, pour concrete, bevel 4" cap.

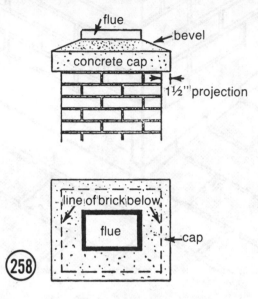

To allow a 1½" projection, nail 1 x 6 to 2 x 4, Illus. 259. Cut sides B to width by length required. Nail sides B to A but don't drive nails all the way. Brace form in position so flue projects 1 to 2" above. Cut 2 x 4's to width and depth of chimney. Nail a clothes line, Illus. 260. Tie 2 x 4 around chimney at height needed to hold form in place. Fill form with cement mortar. Bevel top edge so flue projects above cap.

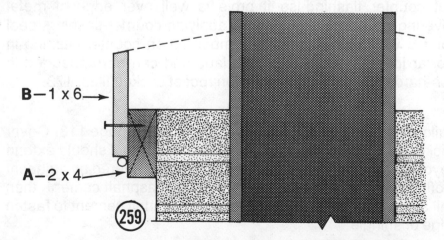

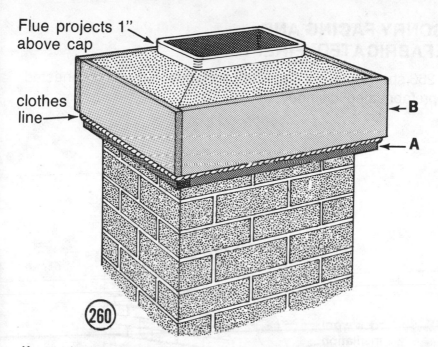

Flue projects 1"
above cap

clothes
line

B

A

(260)

If your house is located in a hollow, or close to trees higher than your house, normal wind currents may cause downdrafts. Under these circumstances play it safe, build chimney up 8 to 12" around flues, Illus. 261, and cap with flagstone, heavy slate, or a precast concrete slab. Slab or cap should project 2" all around. Openings, Illus. 261, should equal the combined area of all flues, Illus. 262.

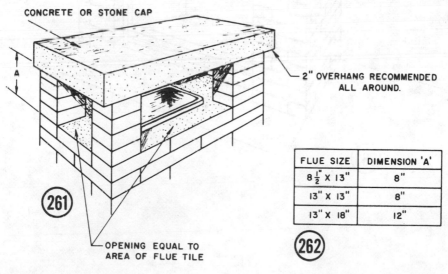

CONCRETE OR STONE CAP

A

2" OVERHANG RECOMMENDED
ALL AROUND.

(261)

OPENING EQUAL TO
AREA OF FLUE TILE

FLUE SIZE	DIMENSION 'A'
$8\frac{1}{2}$" X 13"	8"
13" X 13"	8"
13" X 18"	12"

(262)

171

MASONRY FACING AND PREFABRICATED FIREPLACE

Illus. 263 shows masonry around prefabricated unit connected to a prefabricated chimney.

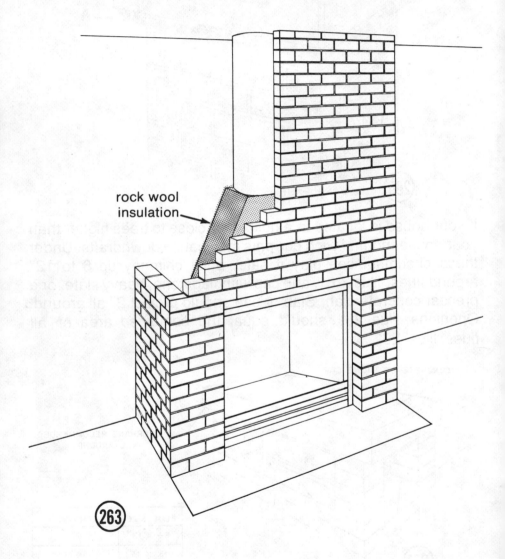

rock wool insulation

(263)

GAS AND ELECTRIC FIREPLACES

The gas fireplace, Illus. 264, has been certified and tested by the American Gas Association; approved by the Canadian Gas Association; Approval #69-10 Building Officials Conference, also bears Research Recommendation No. 2462 of the International Conference of Building Officials.

264

The kind and size of fireplace and where installed is very important. In a city apartment where wood is scarce and costly, a gas or electric fireplace, Illus. 265, adds a romantic touch that's as important as stereo to those who appreciate atmosphere. With a flick of a switch on a wall as far as fifty feet away, a gas fireplace can be turned on as easily as you switch on stereo or dim room lighting. Installation is easy, quick, and depending on gas rates, extremely economical to operate. Gas fireplaces are available for natural gas and LP. The gas fireplace is purely decorative, it doesn't provide any heat. This unit can be cantilevered from a wall, placed in a corner, or recessed.

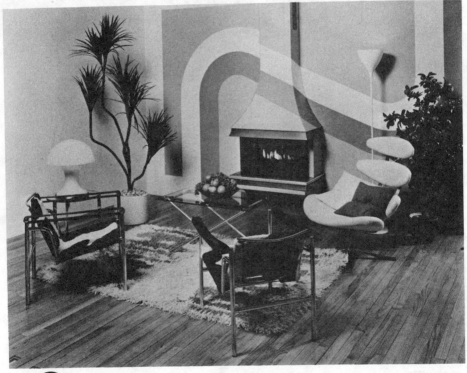

174

Wall hung units can be mounted anywhere it can be properly vented. Floor units can be placed on a finished floor. Illus. 266 shows how a number of units can be vented from a common flue, except the top unit.

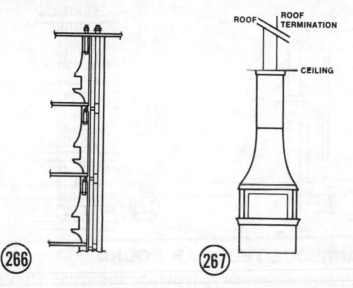

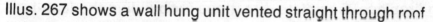

Illus. 267 shows a wall hung unit vented straight through roof

Illus. 268 shows how a unit can be vented between studs using Underwriters' Laboratories listed 5" oval pipe for 2 x 4 venting.

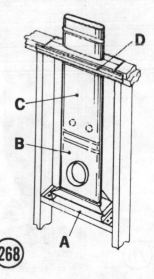

1. Cut ceiling plate where vent is to be installed.

2. Nail 2x4 (A) at height desired between studs.

3. Install tee (B), vent (C) and firestop spacer (D) in space shown.

NOTE

Provide at least 1" clearance around tee branch where it passes through combustible wall construction.

Illus. 269 shows how a through wall pipe can be connected to a single or common vent.

Illus. 270 shows a chimney with a 30° offset.

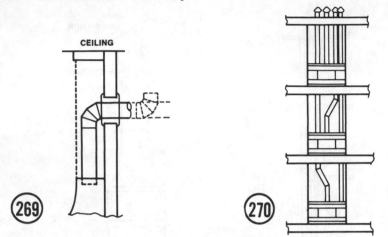

CEILING

(269) (270)

TO BARBECUE THE YEAR ROUND

Build a lean-to alongside your garage and install a free standing fireplace. Complete directions for building the lean-to is described in Book #649.

(271)

ENCLOSURE FOR PREFABRICATED CHIMNEY

If floor space where a prefabricated chimney goes through an upstairs room doesn't provide space for a wall-to-wall clothes closet or stereo cabinet, build a floor-to-ceiling enclosure, Illus. 72.

LIST OF MATERIALS

1 — ¼" x 4' x 8' plywood for B
1 — ¼" x 2' x 8'   "   for E
1 — ⅜" x 4' x 8'   "   for doors
1 — ¾" x 2' x 4'   "   for F
5 — 1 x 2 x 10' for A, C
1 — 1 x 2 x 8' for C
1 — 1 x 3 x 6' for A, D
1 — 1 x 4 x 2' for C
Two dozen ⅝" No. 8 F. H. wood screws
½ lb. 6 penny finishing nails
1 box ⅜" corrugated fasteners
1 box ¾" No. 17 brads
Four cabinet hinges
Two spring catches
One door handle

Fasten 2 x 2 plate to ceiling 2" from chimney in position noted, Illus. 272. Since a floor and/or ceiling frequently slopes, cut all parts to length required.

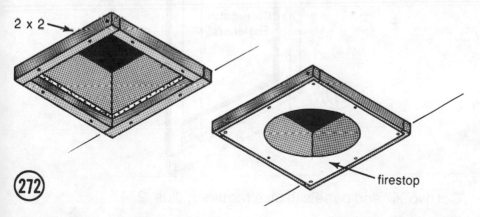

2 x 2

(272)

firestop

177

Assemble two end frames, Illus. 273. Drive two ⅜" corrugated fasteners through from one side, one fastener in from the other side. Toenail frame to floor. Nail frame to plate.

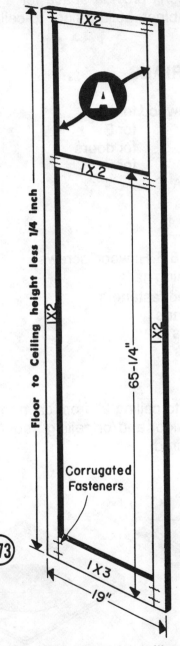

Cut two ¼" end panels to size required, Illus. 274.

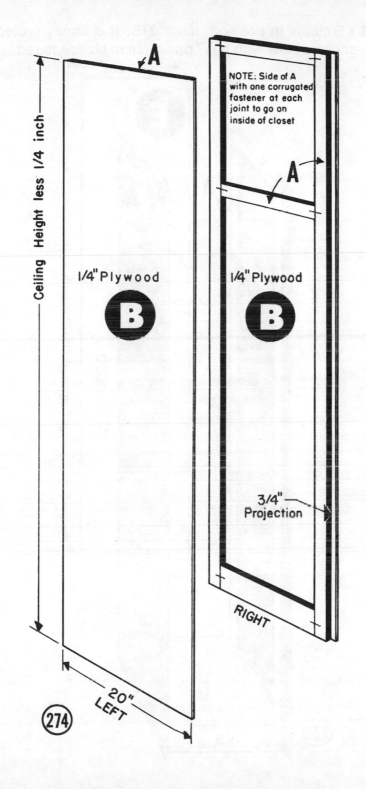

A

NOTE: Side of A with one corrugated fastener at each joint to go on inside of closet

A

1/4" Plywood

B

1/4" Plywood

B

Ceiling Height less 1/4 inch

3/4" Projection

RIGHT

20" LEFT

274

179

Nail 1 x 3 cleats in position, Illus. 275. If chimney projects into room, enclose back with a ¼" panel cut to size required.

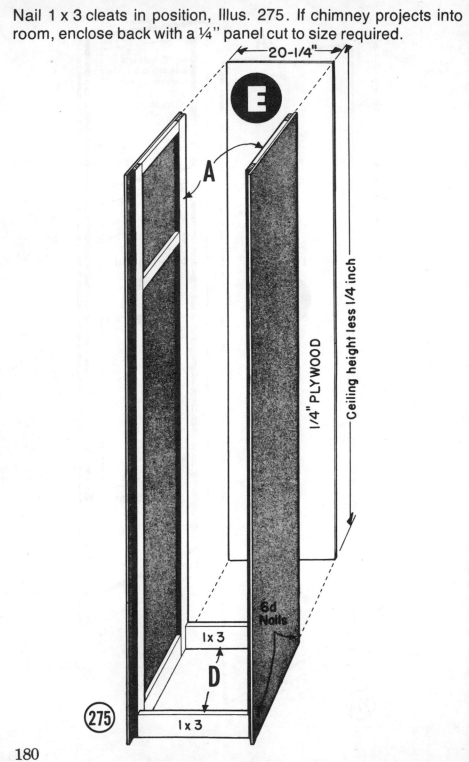

Glue and nail side panels in position shown, Illus. 274, 275, allowing panel to project ¾" in front.

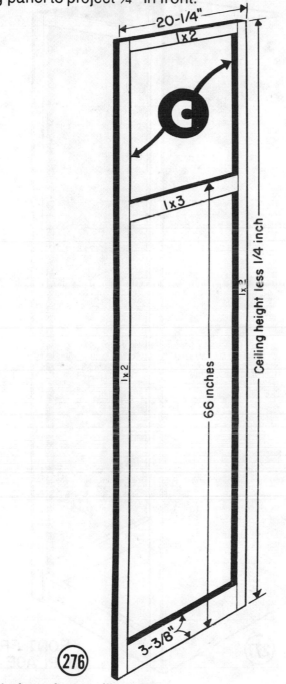

276

Assemble front frame, Illus. 276.

Nail front frame to end frames, Illus. 277.

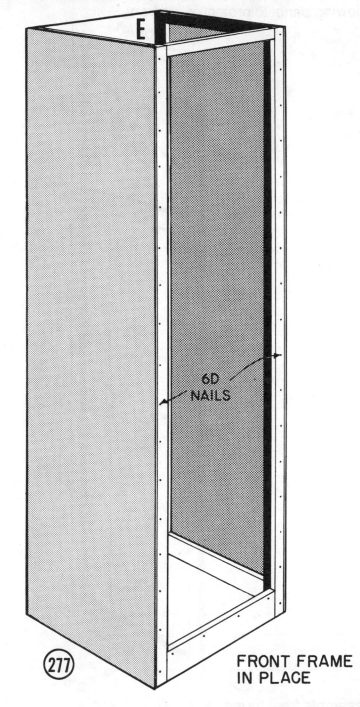

E

6D
NAILS

277

FRONT FRAME
IN PLACE

If you want to add a door, cut one ⅜" plywood panel G, to fit opening, Illus. 278. Saw edge to angle shown, Illus. 279.

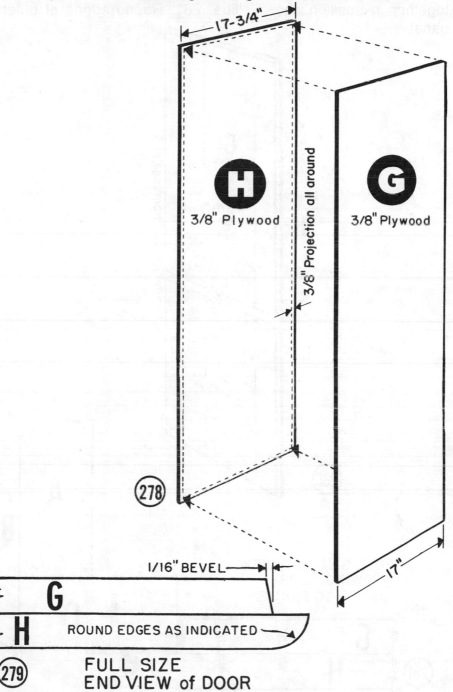

17-3/4"

H

3/8" Plywood

3/8" Projection all around

G

3/8" Plywood

(278)

17"

1/16" BEVEL

G

H

ROUND EDGES AS INDICATED

(279) FULL SIZE
END VIEW of DOOR

Cut another ⅜" panel H, ¾" wider and longer to overlap inner panel ⅜" all around, Illus. 280. Apply glue and screw panels together in position shown, Illus. 281. Round edges of outer panel.

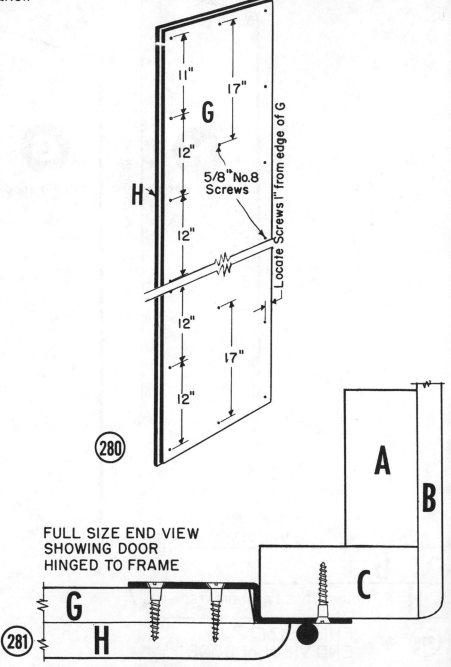

FULL SIZE END VIEW
SHOWING DOOR
HINGED TO FRAME

Hinge door to frame, Illus. 282, using cabinet hinges. Fasten handle in position shown.

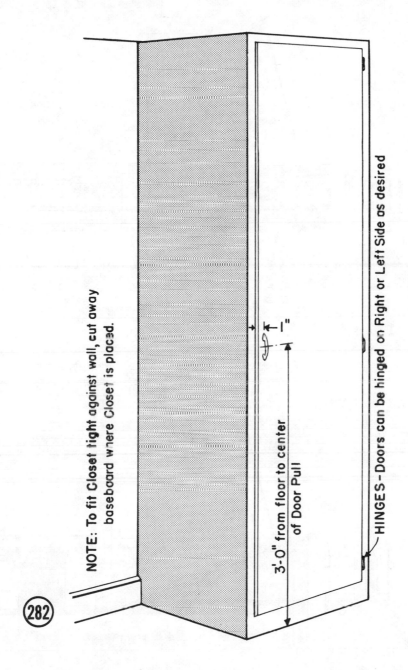

NOTE: To fit Closet tight against wall, cut away baseboard where Closet is placed.

3'-0" from floor to center of Door Pull

1"

HINGES — Doors can be hinged on Right or Left Side as desired

(282)

OUTSIDE ENCLOSURES

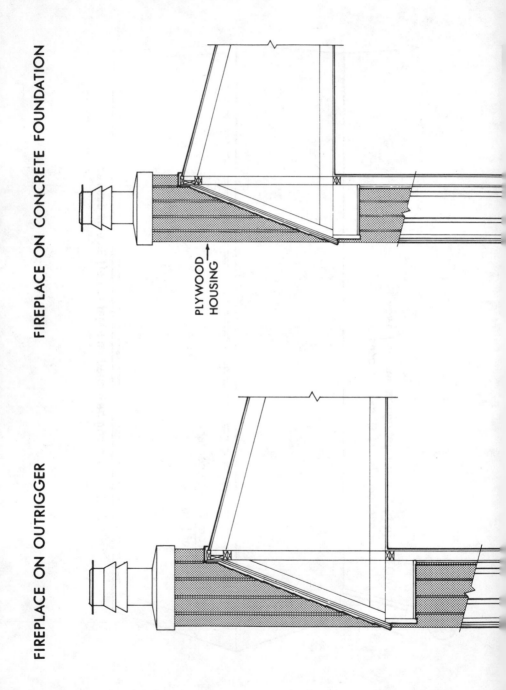

FIREPLACE ON CONCRETE FOUNDATION

PLYWOOD HOUSING

FIREPLACE ON OUTRIGGER

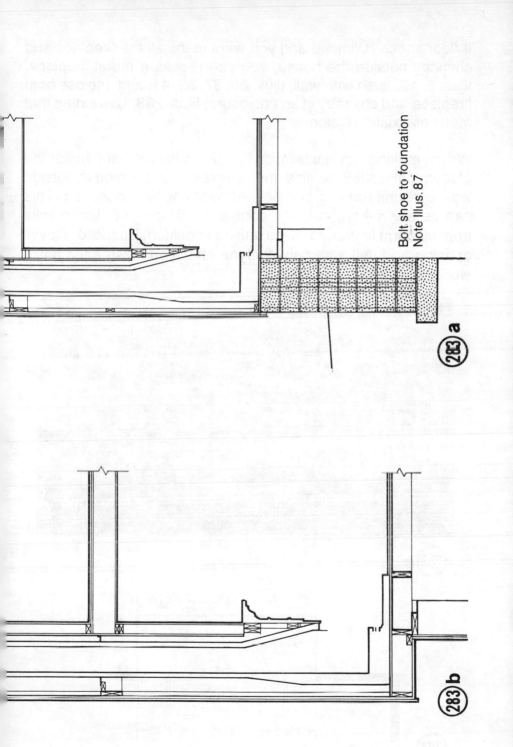

Bolt shoe to foundation
Note Illus. 87

283 a

283 b

If floor space is limited and you want to install the fireplace and chimney outside the house, you can recess a metal fireplace, Illus. 6, 10, flush with wall, Illus. 35, 37, 38, 41, and enclose both fireplace and chimney in an enclosure, Illus. 283. Use siding that matches existing siding.

When making an installation in an outside wall, build the platform,* Illus. 288, to size unit requires. Cut opening in outside wall to permit framing in a header over opening, Illus. 284. This can be a 2 x 4 or 2 x 6 or a double 2 x 6, Illus. 58. Lay planks from platform to ground. Slide unit into position, Illus. 290. Cover opening and unit with polyethelyne after you finish each day's work.

283 a

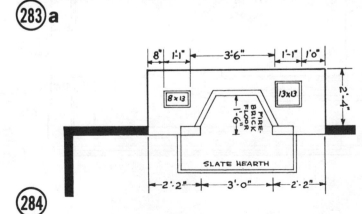

284

*or concrete foundation

188

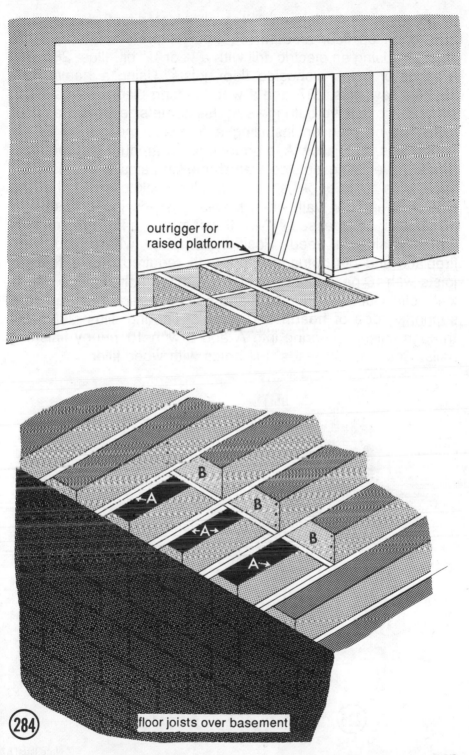

outrigger for
raised platform

284

floor joists over basement

189

If floor joists run at right angle to wall selected for fireplace, Illus. 285, open up floor amount required for prefabricated hearth, Illus. 34. Using an electric drill with a ¼ or ⅜" bit, Illus. 286, drill a series of holes alongside floor joists. Using a heavy duty keyhole saw, Illus. 287, and a wood cutting blade, saw slots in sill beam*to receive outriggers A. Use same size lumber as floor joists. If you plan on installing a fireplace measuring 24" in depth, Illus. 115, allow A to project 24" or amount unit requires. Since the existing outside wall frame contains a 2 x 4 (3½") shoe, plus 1, ¾ or ⅝" sheathing, plus thickness of lathe and plaster on interior wall, when fireplace is positioned flush with inside wall, or recessed ⅜" for tile or.mirror, a 24" projection is normally all you need. Position template where you want fireplace and cut outriggers to length required. Spike to floor joists with 16 penny nails, or drill holes and bolt in place with ⅜ x 4" bolts. Cut solid bridging B and nail in position required so it supports edge of hearth and edge of flooring, Illus. 288. Nail through finished flooring into A and B with 10 penny finishing nails. Countersink heads. Fill holes with wood filler.

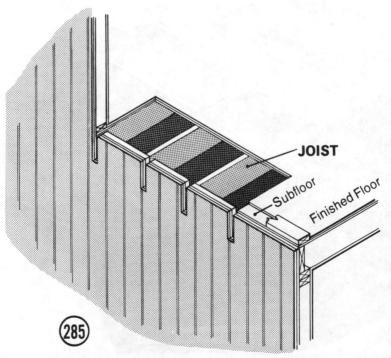

JOIST

Subfloor

Finished Floor

(285)

* Note Illus. 87

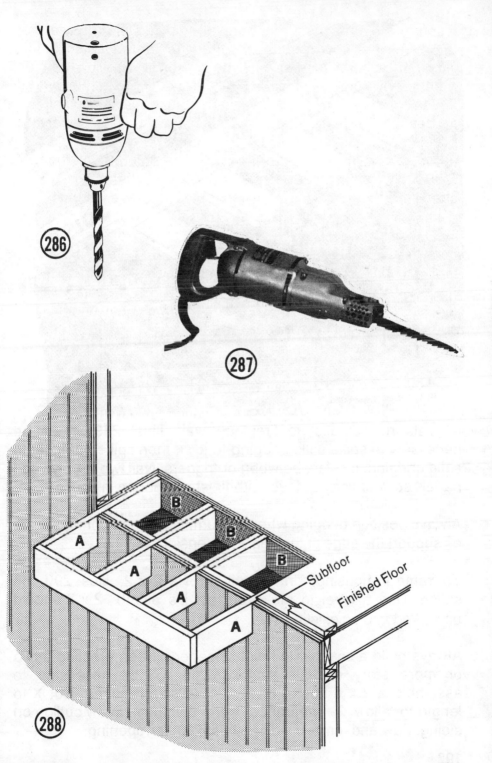

(286)

(287)

(288)

B

B

B

A

A

A

A

A

Subfloor

Finished Floor

191

If joists run parallel to fireplace wall, Illus. 289, it will be necessary to spike solid bridging to joist, then spike outrigger to solid bridging. Insulate between outriggers. Nail two ¾" plywood panels so floor finishes level with finished flooring in house.

Always position bridging where it permits nailing flooring as well as support the edge of the hearth extension.

To frame in housing, draw position of a 2 x 2, Illus. 290, on siding. Use a level to make certain it's plumb. 2 x 2 should be spiked into an existing stud.

Always build a scaffold to height needed. When erecting a two or more story exterior enclosure, it will be necessary to assemble a 2 x 6 frame, Illus. 291, to size required. Cut X to length to allow 2" clearance from chimney. Draw outline on siding. Saw and remove siding, Illus. 291, for opening.

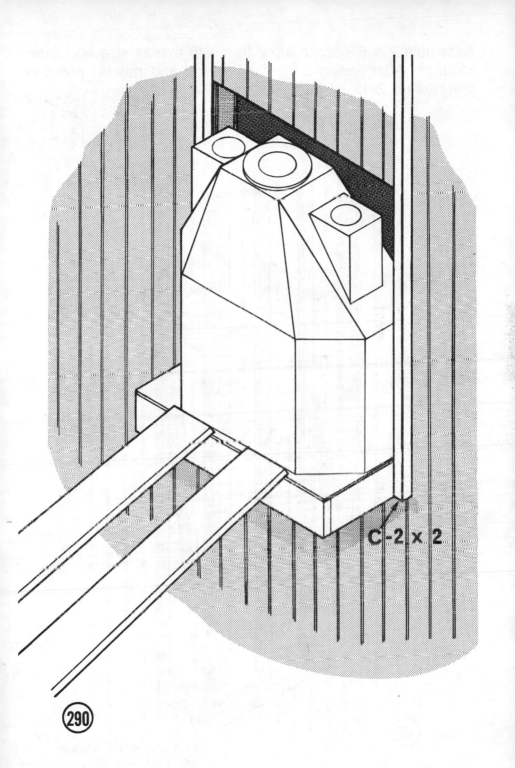

C-2 x 2

(290)

Assemble 2 x 6 second story frame to overall size enclosure requires. After nailing 2 x 6 framing, cut and nail ¼" plywood plates, Illus. 291.

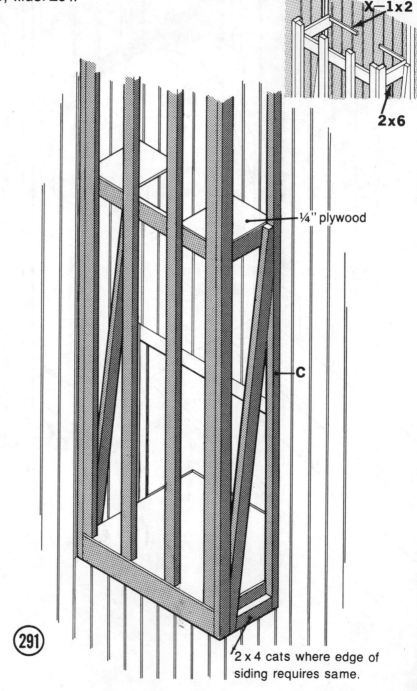

X—1x2

2x6

¼" plywood

C

(291)

2 x 4 cats where edge of siding requires same.

The enclosure can be built to any height required, Illus. 291. To fasten enclosure securely in place and to greatly strengthen platform, drill holes through 2 x 2—C, to receive 16 penny nails. Spike C to outrigger and to house. After positioning fireplace, nail studs in position shown. Cut diagonal corner brace to angle shown, Illus. 291, 292. Nail in position.

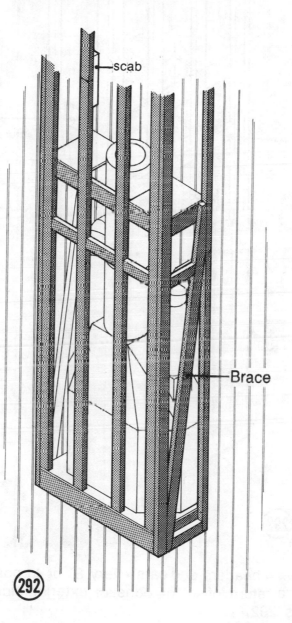

scab

Brace

(292)

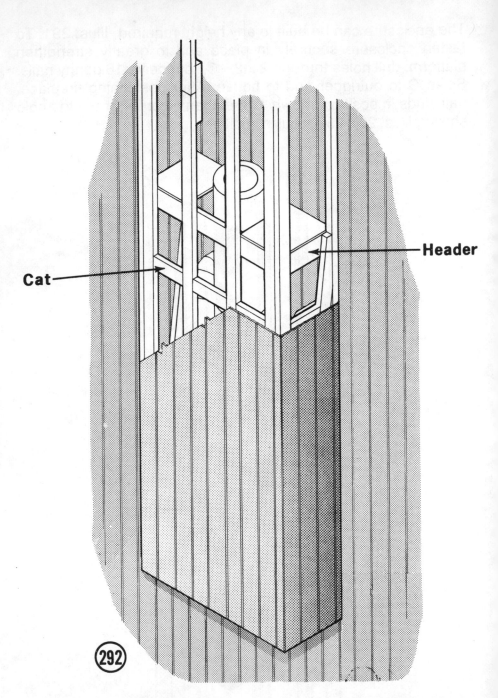

Header

Cat

(292)

Position 2 x 4 headers and cats every 8', or in position where straps on a return offset or edge of exterior siding requires same, Illus. 292.

196

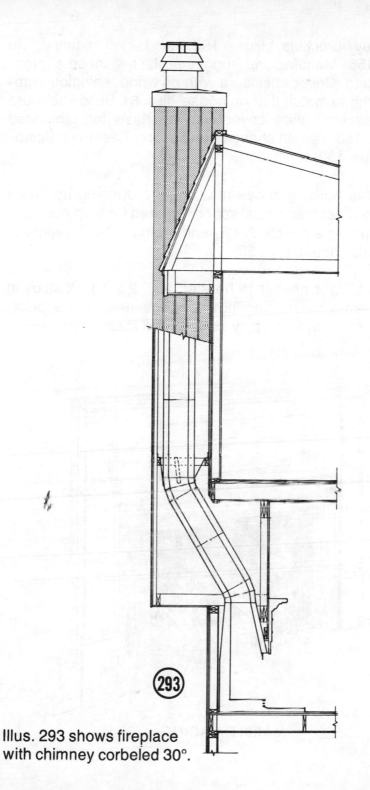

Illus. 293 shows fireplace
with chimney corbeled 30°.

197

Use chimney brackets, Illus. 155, to fasten chimney to house, Illus.156. Manufacturer suggests placing these approximately 9' apart. Cover enclosure with plywood, shingles, clapboard or siding to match that on house, Illus.61. Build enclosure to height required, then cover with a chase top fabricated locally, Illus. 183. Fasten chase to enclosure. Fasten contemporary cap, Illus. 182, in position.

In some areas building codes may require opening up inside wall one stud wider than actual space required for fireplace. This will permit spiking a double 2 x 6, and a single 2 x 4 header to studs in position noted, Illus. 58.

Toe nail studs over header to header. Nail 2 x 4 jack studs in position shown. This framing now permits nailing sheetrock. Tape joints, paint wall or apply brick or tile facing.

MARBLE FACING

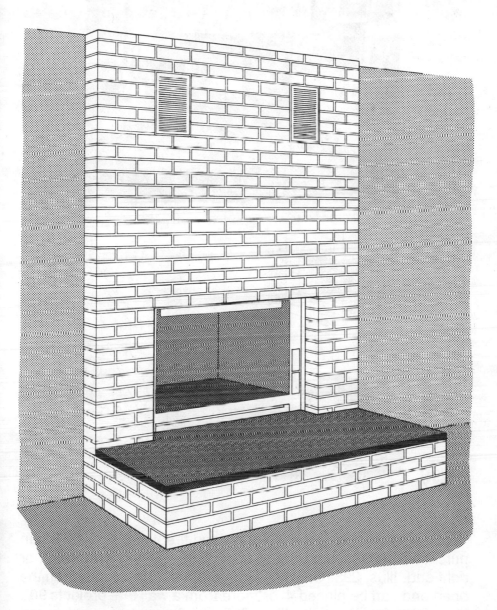

BRICK FACED FIREPLACE WITH RAISED HEARTH

OPEN END FIREPLACE

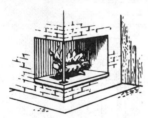

(294)

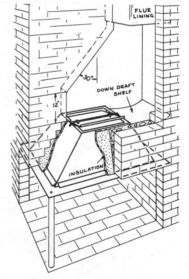

Those who want to install an open end fireplace, Illus. 294, can purchase prefabricated metal units with opening on the left or right end, Illus. 295. Only install an open end fireplace when the open end can be placed 4' or more from a wall that projects 90°, Illus. 296. A wall shield, Illus. 297, available on special order, should be fastened to wall in positions shown, Illus. 296. Note how extra hearth extension is placed in front of open end.

Chimney
9″ I.D.
14″ O.D.

56½″

36½″

24″

41″

(295)

Left Side Open

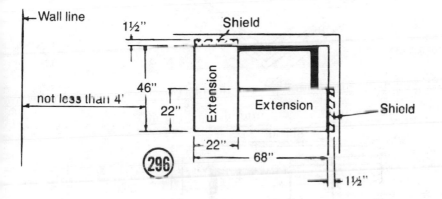

←Wall line

Shield

1½″

46″

not less than 4′

22″

Extension

Extension

Shield

22″

68″

1½″

(296)

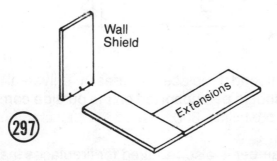

Wall
Shield

Extensions

(297)

In some cases, especially when heavy stone is used to face a fireplace wall, a special lintel is required, Illus. 298. Brick facing over a masonry fireplace is easily supported by the wide flange on the universal damper, Illus. 299.

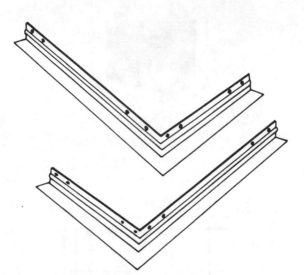

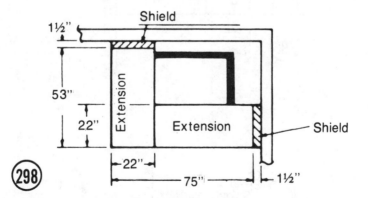

(298)

A masonry open end fireplace requires a universal damper, Illus. 299. This should be supported on the outside corner with a round or square post, Illus. 300.

The universal damper is also required for fireplaces that open in two adjoining rooms, Illus. 301; or on three faces, Illus. 302.

202

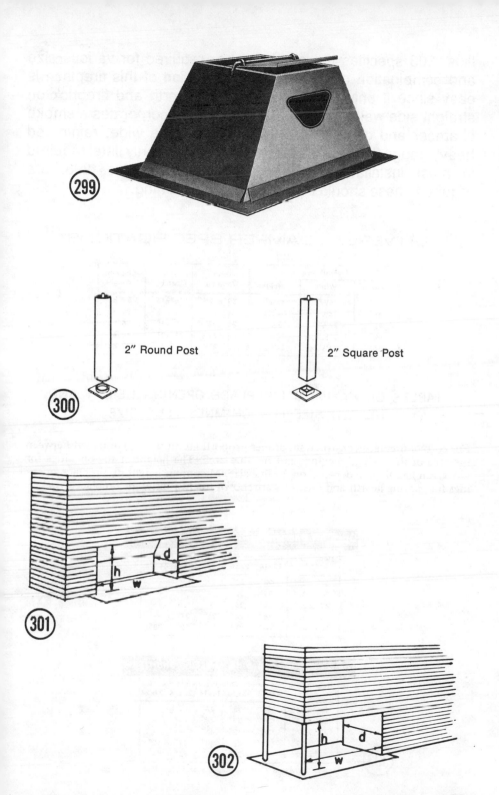

Illus. 303 specifies universal damper required for various size and combination of openings. Construction of this fireplace is easy since it only requires a firebrick hearth and firebrick on straight side walls. The universal damper incorporates a smoke chamber and damper in one unit. The extra wide, reinforced heavy gauge flange around the damper is the only lintel required in most installations. When special lintels, Illus. 298, are required, these should be lag screwed to framing.

UNIVERSAL DAMPER SPECIFICATIONS

Overall Size			Base Opening	Top Opening	Shipping Weight
Length	Width	Height			
37″	26½″	12¼″	30″x19½″	16″x16″	72 lbs.
41″	28½″	14″	34″x21½″	18″x18″	85 lbs.
45″	29½″	17½″	38″x22½″	18″x18″	96 lbs.
49″	31½″	18¼″	42″x24½″	21″x21″	148 lbs.
57″	34½″	22½″	50″x27½″	24″x24″	200 lbs.

TABLES OF MAXIMUM FIREPLACE OPENING HEIGHT AND HEARTH SIZE FOR CHIMNEY FLUE SIZE

For correct fireplace construction, proper proportions must be maintained between the area of the firebox openings and the flue area. The height of the openings for any given hearth area depends on the flue size. Maximum height of fireplace openings for varying hearth and flue sizes are shown for five different fireplace types.

Open on One Short Side and Two Long Sides

Hearth Size	Maximum Opening Height for Flue				
	13x18	18x18	20x24	24x24	24 dia.
34″ x 28″	23″	28″	—	—	—
38″ x 30″	21″	28″	—	—	—
42″ x 31″	19″	26″	—	—	—
46″ x 33″	18″	24″	31″	37″	—
54″ x 36″	—	21″	27″	32″	38″

Open on One Long Side and One Short Side

Hearth Size	Maximum Opening Height for Flue				
	13x13	13x18	18x18	20x24	24x24
34″ x 24″	*26″	38″	47″	—	—
38″ x 26″	*23″	35″	47″	—	—
42″ x 27″	*20″	32″	43″	—	—
46″ x 29″	*19″	29″	40″	52″	62″
54″ x 32″	—	26″	35″	45″	54′

*May be increased 2″ if chimney is over 17 feet high.

Open on One Long Side and Two Short Sides

Hearth Size	Maximum Opening Height for Flue				
	13x18	18x18	20x24	24x24	24 dia.
38" x 24"	26"	32"	—	—	—
42" x 26"	24"	32"	—	—	—
46" x 27"	22"	30"	—	—	—
50" x 29"	21"	28"	36"	43"	—
58" x 32"	18"	25"	32"	38"	45"

Openings in Two Adjoining Rooms

Hearth Size	Maximum Opening Height for Flue				
	13x13	13x18	18x18	20x24	24x24
30" x 28"	*24"	37"	45"	—	—
34" x 30"	*22"	32"	44"	—	—
38" x 31"	*19"	29"	39"	—	—
42" x 33"	—	26"	36"	46"	55"
50" x 36"	—	22"	30"	38"	46"

*May be increased 2" if chimney is over 17 feet high.

Opening on All Four Sides

Hearth Size	Maximum Opening Height for Flue				
	13x18	18x18	20x24	24x24	24 dia.
38" x 28"	17"	21"	—	—	—
42" x 30"	—	21"	—	—	—
46" x 31"	—	19"	—	—	—
50" x 33"	—	18"	23"	28"	—
58" x 36"	—	—	21"	25"	29"

(303)

Illus. 304 shows position of smoke shelf and flue in relation to damper over a left end open fireplace. Smoke shelf can be positioned to the right, left or rear.

The universal damper helps insure satisfactory operation of a fireplace when dimensions shown in Illus. 294, 303, are followed. Proper proportions must be maintained between the area of the firebox and the area of flue. The purpose of this book is to alert the reader to those areas where improvisation should be avoided. The hearth size, and opening height, plus size of flue area are all related. You can't alter one dimension without lousing up the efficiency of the unit.

The universal damper, Illus. 299, comes with a roll of insulation. Cover damper with insulation following manufacturer's directions. Check the damper control chains to make certain they are free. Make certain damper blade moves easily yet sufficiently tight to hold in any position required. Tighten or loosen nuts on both ends of blade.

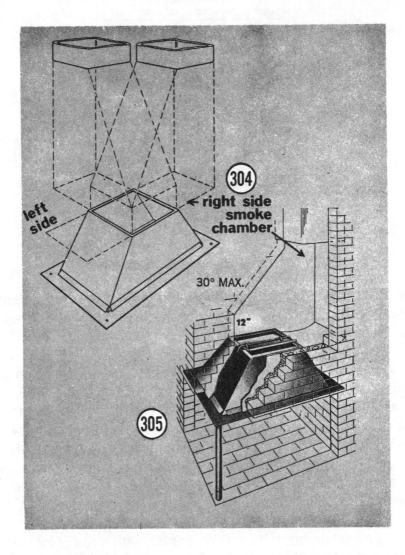

left side

(304) → right side smoke chamber

30° MAX.

12"

(305)

Build sides and back of firebox with firebrick to dimensions shown, Illus. 303, 305. Use ⅛" fireclay joints on hearth, up to ⅜" on sides and back. Position damper on masonry at height specified. Install a corner support, Illus. 300, on unsupported corner. If you don't want to buy a corner post, a length of 1¼" to 1½" cast iron pipe, filled with concrete can be used. Anchor a 20 penny nail in mortar in bottom. Allow nail to project 1¼" to 1½".

Either drill hole in firebrick or insert nail in fireclay joint. Place a 10 or 16 penny nail through lip of damper into wet mortar in pipe to lock pipe in position. Check pipe with level.

Position flue at height above damper as specified, Illus. 303. The flue should be placed to right, or left or to the rear as dash lines, Illus. 304, indicates, but never directly over damper.

Slope of smoke chamber should not exceed 30°.

The downdraft shelf should be laid in mortar as wide as the damper and extend back to a straight wall directly in line with flue. Slope both ends of the shelf as it meets damper and wall. Shelf can finish 1" below top edge of damper.

Fill in front and back of damper with sufficient mortar to support bricks on chimney. Try not to crush insulation anymore than by weight of concrete.

To provide clearance for damper blade, masonry should extend straight up for a distance of 12" from top of damper. It can then start to be corbeled over to the flue. Do not exceed 30° from vertical.

INSTALLING FANS AND GRILLE (OPTIONAL)

Always install fans in cold air inlet, Illus. 57, never in hot air outlet. Position fan housing so it projects amount required to fit flush with exterior wall finish, Illus. 26. Fasten housing to framing in position required.

Remove screw holding cover, Illus. 306. Punch out hole in bottom and back, Illus. 306. Fasten wires from both fans with BX, white to white, black to black, Illus. 307. Use wire nuts. Connect black B from fans to a wall switch near fireplace, then continue black A to a live black connected to a wall outlet. The white line can be connected to white in switch outlet.

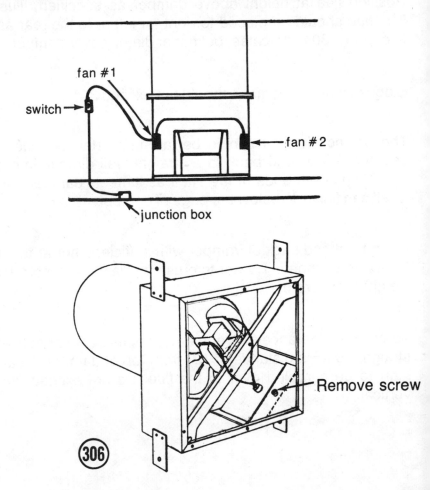

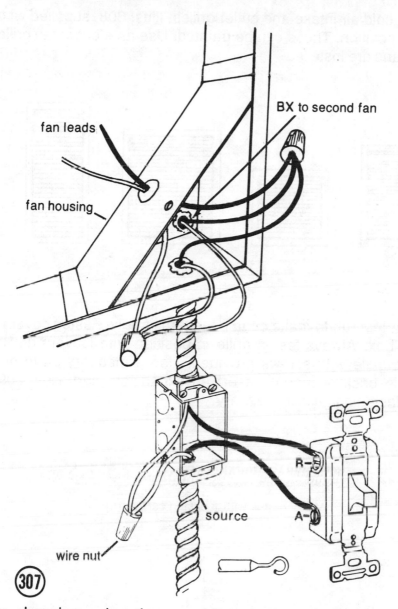

fan leads

BX to second fan

fan housing

source

R—

A—

wire nut

(307)

In choosing a location consider whether any wiring to base outlets will need to be rerouted. In some cases you can disconnect wire at one box and snake in a longer length. This can be laid around back of unit. Or nail an extra box to inside of framing. Cut existing wire so it can be joined inside box with a new length to base outlet. Book #694 Easi-Bild Simplifies Electrical Repairs contains much helpful information.

Fasten cold air intake and outlet grilles, Illus. 308, supplied with unit, in position. These can be painted. Use an electric fan grille when fans are installed.

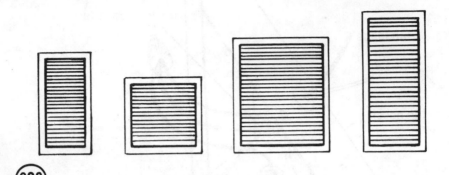

(308)

Make a test run to make certain fan turns freely. Fasten cover to wiring box. Always fasten grille in position with louvers down. Fasten grille with screws provided. Use a masonry bit to drill holes in brick or mortar. Insert an expansion plug, Illus. 309, when fastening grille to masonry.

Masonry drill with tungsten carbide tip.

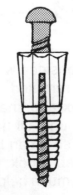

(309)

HOW TO BUILD A FIREPLACE MANTEL

Some hot air circulating fireplaces, with the cold air intake and hot air outlets on front, Illus. 310, permit building a mantel with hinged doors. Open door before starting fire. You can build a mantel for a 36" wide opening with materials noted.

Paneling a fireplace wall adds much to room decor while a mantel, Illus. 310, constructed of matching hardwood plywood adds great charm. Since many fireplaces contain metal air chambers that draw cold air through openings at floor level, and discharge warm air through top ports, the mantel must contain openings, Illus. 311,* to size and position required. Hinged doors conceal openings when fireplace isn't in use, Illus. 310.

* If hot air circulating unit is installed.

LIST OF MATERIALS

1—¾ x 30 x 72" plywood for Parts 1 and 2
1—1 x 8 x 12 ft. for Parts 3, 5 and 6
1—1 x 3 x 6 ft. for Part 4
1—5/4 x 8 x 4 ft. for Part 7, 8
8 ft. ¾ x 2½" Door Trim Molding No. 9
8 ft. 1¾ x 2" Crown Molding No. 11
3 ft. ¾" nosing No. 12
½ lb. 8 Penny finishing nails
¼ lb. 4 Penny finishing nails
1 box 1¼" No. 17 brads
Glue
4 prs. 1 x 1½" tight pin butt hinges for doors
14 lineal feet Molding for #10
3 lineal feet Molding for #13
3 lineal feet Molding for #14

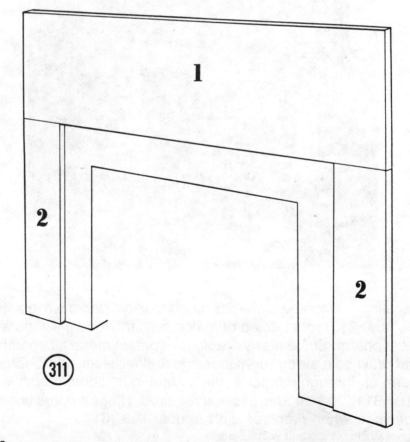

Illus. 311 shows parts 1 and 2 of a mantel for a radiant heat metal fireplace, Illus. 6, or a masonry firebox, Illus. 51.

Illus. 312 shows a mantel without hinged doors.

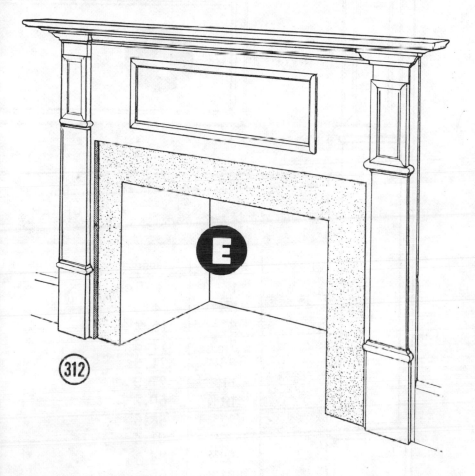

(312)

To simplify step-by-step construction, directions explain how to build a mantel for a 36" wide by 27" opening, Illus. 313. We allowed 5½" around opening for slate, tile or exposed brick. Alter parts 1 and 2, Illus. 313, to fit your fireplace. The metric dimensions are approximate and are offered only as a general guide.

The mantel shown, Illus. 313, is 52¾ x 68¼" wide.

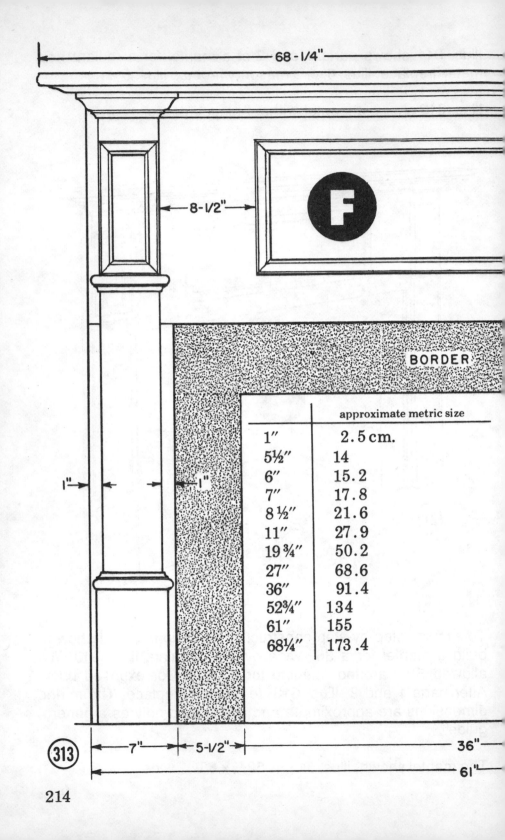

68 - 1/4"

8 - 1/2"

F

BORDER

	approximate metric size
1"	2.5 cm.
5½"	14
6"	15.2
7"	17.8
8 ½"	21.6
11"	27.9
19 ¾"	50.2
27"	68.6
36"	91.4
52¾"	134
61"	155
68¼"	173 .4

1"

1"

313

7"

5-1/2"

36"

61"

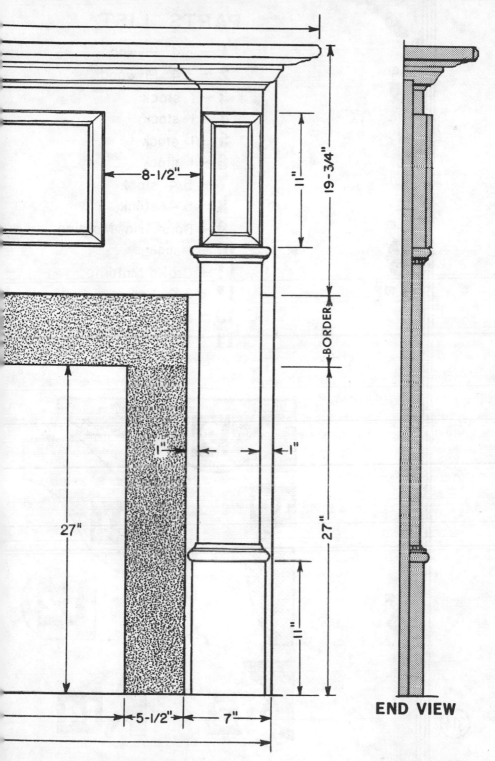

8-1/2"

19-3/4"

11"

BORDER

1"← →← →← 1"

27"

27"

11"

5-1/2" 7"

END VIEW

215

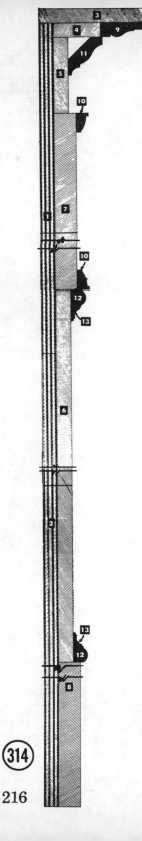

PARTS LIST

1 — 3/4" Plywood
2 — 3/4" Plywood
3 — 1" stock
4 — 1" stock
5 — 1" stock
6 — 1" stock
7 — 5/4" stock
8 — 5/4" stock
9 — Door Trim Molding
10 — Molding
11 — Crown Molding
12 — 3/4" Nosing
13 — Molding
14 — Molding

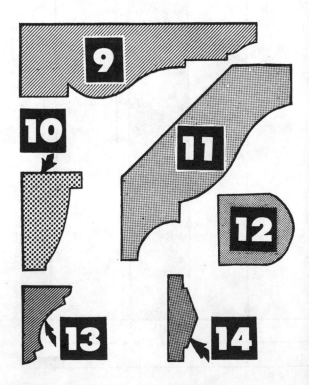

Illus. 314 shows location of each numbered part and material used. It also shows full size end view of moldings used on sample mantel. All materials are available in lumber yards. If ¾" matching hardwood plywood is available, it can be used for parts 1 and 2. Or you can use ¾" fir plywood and stain it to match paneling on wall; or use ½" fir plywood and cover with ¼" hardwood plywood that matches paneling.

Cut part 1, Illus. 315, 19" wide by length required. The length of part 1 is estimated by adding width of fireplace opening (36") plus two borders 11", plus 14".

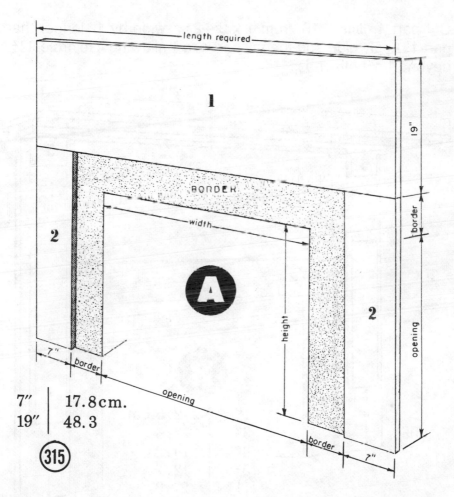

7"	17.8 cm.
19"	48.3

(315)

Cut part 2, 7" wide, by length equal to fireplace opening, plus width of top border. All other parts are cut to size noted regardless of any change in size of parts 1 and 2.

Apply glue and fasten parts 1 and 2 in position using ½ x 1½" corrugated fasteners driven in back face. Allow glue to set. Place assembled 1 and 2 in position. Check with level and nail in place with 8 penny finishing nails driven into studs.

Cut part 3 from 1 x 8 to 5⅝" width, Illus. 316, to length of part 1, plus 6". This allows 3" projection on each side. Apply glue and nail in position to top edge of part 1 with 8 penny finishing nails.

Cut part 4, Illus. 316, from 1 x 3—2⅜" wide by 1" longer than part 1. Apply glue and toenail part 4 to 1 allowing 4 to project ½" beyond 1 at both ends.

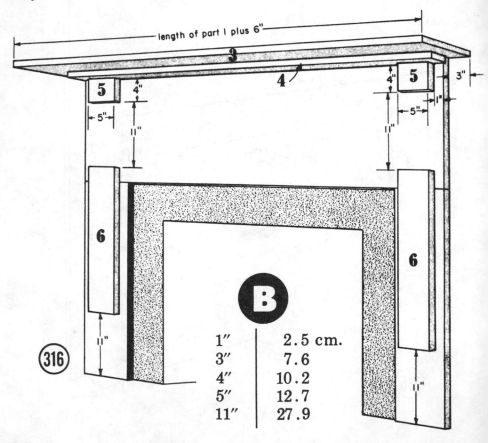

B	
1"	2.5 cm.
3"	7.6
4"	10.2
5"	12.7
11"	27.9

Cut two parts 5, Illus. 316, from 1 x 8—5" wide by 4" long. Apply glue and nail in position with 4 penny finishing nails. Part 5 is recessed 1" from edge of part 1.

Locate and mark position of part 6, Illus. 316. Locate 6—11" below part 5 and 11" up from bottom. Cut two pieces 5" wide by length required. Glue, nail or hinge #6, 1" in from edge of part 2.

Cut two pieces of 5/4 x 8" to 5 x 11" for part 7, Illus. 317. Nail part 7 in position shown with 4 penny finishing nails. If fireplace outlet or cold air inlet is under part 6 or 8, hinge 6 or 8 with 1 x 1½" tight pin hinges.

Cut two pieces of 5/4 x 8 to 6 x 11" for part 8, Illus. 317. Glue and nail in position ½" in from edge of part 2 using 4 penny finishing nails or hinge in position as noted above.

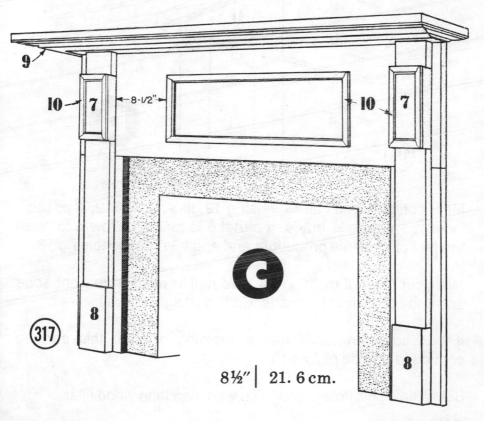

8½" | 21. 6 cm.

Miter cut molding 9, Illus. 314, 317, same length as 3. Apply glue and nail in position with 1¼" brads. Position 9 flush with front edge of 3. Miter cut one end of two additional 5⅝" lengths of same molding. Apply glue and nail in position at ends, Illus. 317.

Miter cut four pieces of molding 10, Illus. 317, to 11", 4 pieces 5". Apply glue and nail in position with 1¼" brads. Miter cut two additional 11" lengths. Nail in position for center panel. Miter cut two pieces to length required and nail in place.

Miter cut, glue and nail crown molding 11, Illus. 314, 318, 319, with 1¼" brads. Fasten long length in place, then cut shorter pieces to fit. Molding 11 butts against wall. It is notched to fit around 1, Illus. 319.

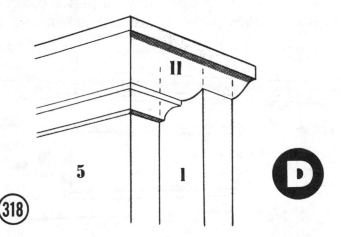

Miter cut, glue and nail ¾" nosing 12, Illus. 314, 319, in position indicated with 1¼" brads. If panel 6 is hinged, allow 6 to open freely. Follow same procedure and apply ½" cove molding 13.

Miter cut ends of molding 14, and nail in position to front edge and ends of 3 with 1¼" brads. Ends butt against wall.

If baseboard in room has a molding on top, this can be continued up side of 2 and 1.

Set all nails. Fill holes. Touch up with matching wood filler.

If 5/4" lumber is difficult to obtain, use 1" lumber and cover with ¼" prefinished plywood.

If the metal grille on cold air inlet doesn't permit fastening part 2 against wall, mortise out back of 2 about 3/16" deep to receive grille. Don't permit wood to come in direct contact with metal. Cover edge of mortise with a strip of sheet asbestos.

When hinging 6, mortise edge to receive full thickness of hinge. Doors can be held in closed position with a bullet type door catch.

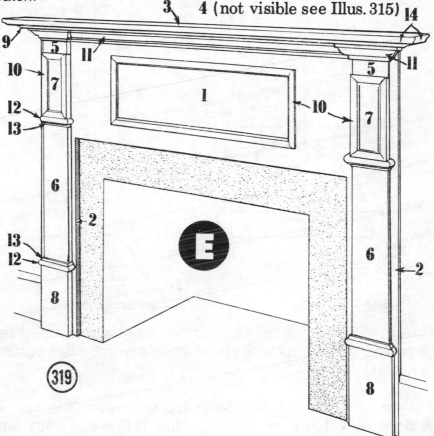

Book #606 How to Lay Ceramic Tile contains much helpful information. Read this book if you want to apply tile around fireplace opening, or cover the entire face of a fireplace wall with colorful, easy to clean ceramic tile.

FREE STANDING FIREPLACE

A log burning, free standing fireplace, Illus. 5, 320, that takes logs up to 20", is not only easy to install, fun to use, but also a sound home improvement investment. If you decide to turn a basement into a family room or transform a garage into a rentable living unit, a free standing fireplace creates an atmosphere that's hard to equal.

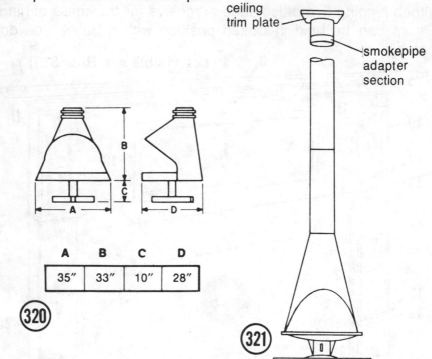

A	B	C	D
35"	33"	10"	28"

The entire unit, fireplace, base, smoke stack and chimney, can be purchased as a complete package in several colors besides flatte black.

The fireplace comes with a base and firescreen. You get two sections of matching smokepipe, Illus. 321, and a smokepipe adapter, the same color as fireplace. This, plus a ceiling trim plate, Illus. 110, fits an 8' ceiling installation.

Where you have a cathedral ceiling, or one more than 8', just measure height and order additional length smokepipe.

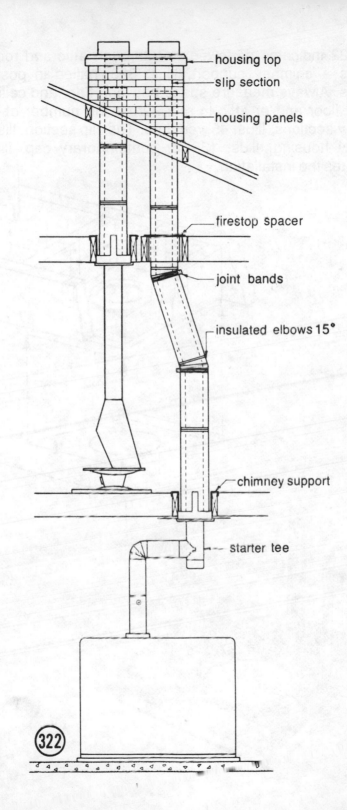

housing top

slip section

housing panels

firestop spacer

joint bands

insulated elbows 15°

chimney support

starter tee

322

Illus. 322 indicates parts required through attic and roof. This requires a chimney support, Illus. 323, nailed in position to headers. Always measure space between floor and ceiling of a second floor and/or attic to roof. Order the number of 2' or 3' chimney sections, Illus. 45, required. The slip section, Illus. 151, chimney housing, Illus. 136, or contemporary cap, Illus. 81, completes the installation.

A smokepipe adapter, Illus. 324, simplifies making a connection between smokepipe and chimney.

SMOKEPIPE ADAPTER

(324)   9" SMOKEPIPE

The unit can be placed anywhere you find it convenient, providing you keep the back of the unit at least 20" from a wall, and all combustible surfaces. Keep furniture 28" away on sides. To obtain the most efficient operation, position fireplace close to chimney. Keep the smokepipe connection short. Do not connect this unit to a flue serving the furnace or any other fireplace. The smokepipe must also be positioned 18" or more from combustible material. When you have selected the location desired, plan on fastening the base to the floor. A hole in base, Illus. 325, permits fastening to floor with ¼ x 1" lag screw.

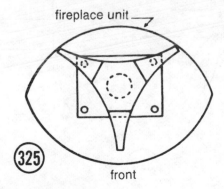

fireplace unit

(325)

front

The floor around these free standing fireplaces, plus 8" on either side, and 16" in front should be brick, concrete, or other noncombustible material. A circular hearth ring, Illus. 326, can be placed around unit and filled with white stone chips or gravel. Or you can lay out brick dry or use heavy flagstone.

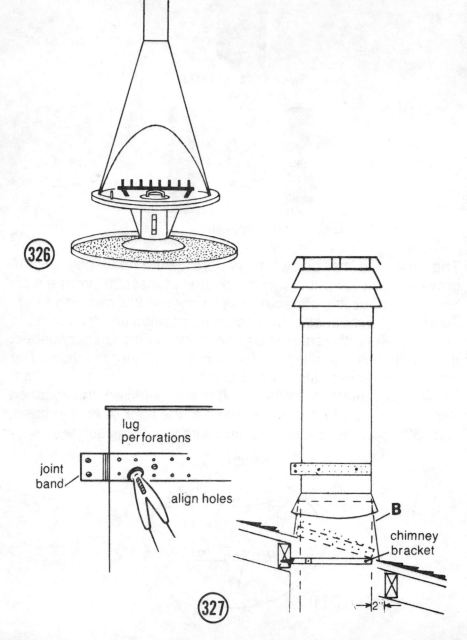

The contemporary chimney comes complete with a cap A, chimney cover plate B, storm collar C, flashing cone D, two flashing halves E, Illus. 81. On steep pitched roofs, the flashing halves come through with a center extender plate. This chimney can project up to 7' above low side. It should extend at least 2' higher than any portion of the building within 10', Illus. 327.

The flashing cone B has lines that indicate where to cut cone to fit various roof pitches, Illus. 81. Use aviation snips or a metal cutting keyhole saw.

The flashing halves are marked low and high side. Position low side, then let high side overlap low side, Illus. 328.

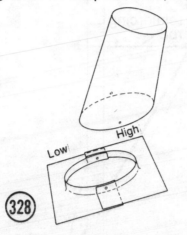

After framing opening in roof 18 x 18 for a 9" chimney, or 15½ x 15½ for a 7" chimney, the chimney bracket is nailed in position, Illus. 155, 327. Joint bands, Illus. 124, are fastened with bolts holding bands positioned toward ridge.

Place cone over flashing. Pull halves apart until they fasten tight against inside of cone.

Drill two ⅛" holes through each side of cone and fasten cone to flashing with ½" screws manufacturer provides.

Nail flashing to roof with 1½" neoprene roofing nails supplied. Calk around flashing with asphalt cement.

Install chimney cover by twisting clockwise to last section of chimney. Install cap A and fasten in position with locking bolt. Then drill two ⅛" holes and fasten in place with two screws supplied.

If chimney projects high above roof, Illus. 329, it should be windproofed with ¾ or 1" rods. You can use electrical conduit pipe with ends flattened. Drill a hole through each end and bolt rod to joint band and to a 2 x 2 nailed to roof.

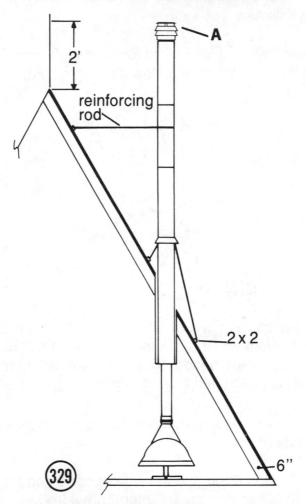

If you install a horizontal smokepipe, keep horizontal length half or less than the length of the vertical chimney. A horizontal smokepipe should rise at least ¼" per foot, Illus. 330.

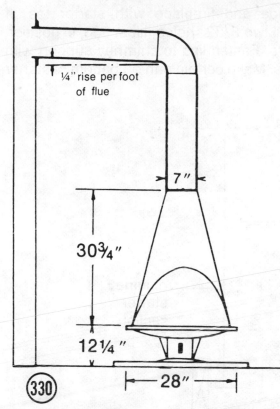

¼" rise per foot of flue

7"

30¾"

12¼"

28"

(330)

If you want to connect a horizontal smokepipe to a chimney, use an elbow, Illus. 331, available in colors to match smokepipe, and a starter tee, Illus. 332.

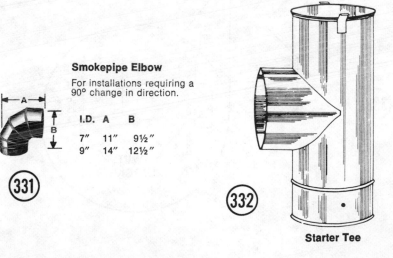

Smokepipe Elbow

For installations requiring a 90° change in direction.

I.D.	A	B
7"	11"	9½"
9"	14"	12½"

(331)

(332)

Starter Tee

Check line of smokepipe and fireplace with starter tee. If everything works out, drill two 3/32" holes, Illus. 333, in position lips on starter tee require. Fasten lips to chimney support with ½" stainless steel screws. Make certain pan on bottom of starter tee is securely fastened.

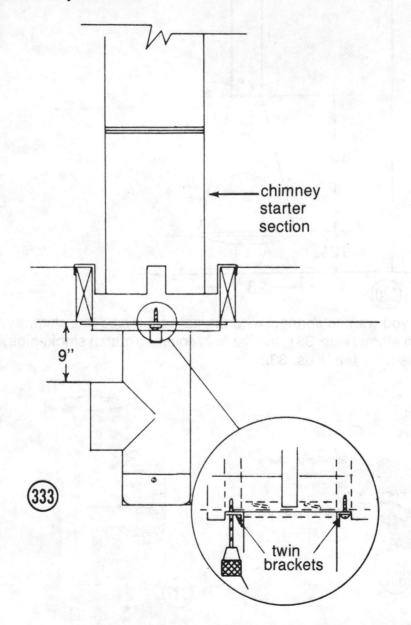

chimney
starter
section

9"

333

twin
brackets

Since codes require most heating units be positioned a minimum of 18" from a combustible surface, many building inspectors will approve an installation when sheet asbestos is applied to ceiling, Illus. 334. Suspend 28 gauge sheet metal 1" below the asbestos. The National Building Code recommended by the American Insurance Association considers shielding shown in Illus. 334, acceptable. Drill ¼" holes through corners of metal. Using 2" screws, drive screws into joists in ceiling about ¾". Allow metal to hang on heads of screws about 1¼" below ceiling. Installation must be made according to recommendations by the building inspector.

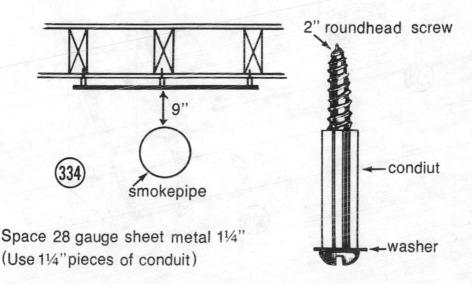

2" roundhead screw

9"

(334)

smokepipe

← condiut

← washer

Space 28 gauge sheet metal 1¼"
(Use 1¼" pieces of conduit)

When connecting a vertical smokepipe to a chimney, Illus. 321, insert the smaller end of a smokepipe adapter, Illus. 324, into the insulated chimney section. Use sufficient smokepipe and/or matching smokepipe elbows, Illus. 331, so top of adapter extends at least 2" into chimney after adapter has been pulled down to connect to smokepipe.

Illus. 323 shows chimney support fastened to headers.

231

Illus. 335 shows a studio support. This requires roof framing following manufacturer's directions, Illus. 336. This greatly simplifies installation of a free standing fireplace, Illus. 329, in an A-frame building. The opening in roof is cut and framed to size noted, Illus. 337, for a 7 or 9" flue.

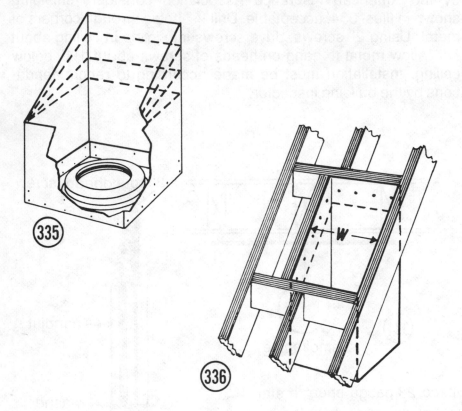

335

336

STUDIO SUPPORT		
SIZE	"W"	ROOF PITCH
7"	15 1/2"	Flat to 12/12
7"	15 1/2"	12/12 to 24/12
9"	18"	Flat to 12/12
9"	18"	12/12 to 24/12

337

The studio support is nailed in plumb position, Illus. 338.

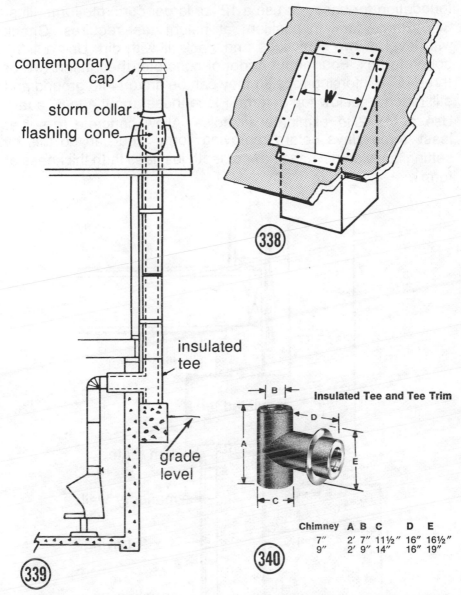

contemporary cap

storm collar

flashing cone

W

338

insulated tee

grade level

Insulated Tee and Tee Trim

B

D

A

E

C

Chimney	A	B	C	D	E
7″	2′	7″	11½″	16″	16½″
9″	2′	9″	14″	16″	19″

339

340

The smokepipe, Illus. 321, and smokepipe adapter, Illus. 324, are used between fireplace and studio support.

When installing a unit in a basement playroom, with the chimney outside, Illus. 339, use an insulated tee, Illus. 340.

233

Cut hole through concrete block or masonry wall to size tee requires. Excavate to depth below frost level and lay a masonry foundation for base, or use a 12" or larger concrete form, Illus. 341. Brace form in position, at height tee requires. Check with level in two directions and back fill with dirt. Use a 1-3-5 concrete mix. Pour about a foot of concrete, then insert two or three ½" reinforcing rods so they can be driven into ground and still reach 1" below top of form. Place these about 4 to 6" apart. Use a 1 x 2 to eliminate air holes. Allow concrete to set at least three days before removing form. You can do this by setting an electric hand saw to depth just less than thickness of form.

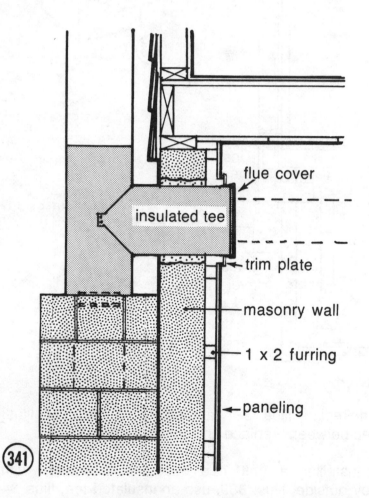

flue cover

insulated tee

trim plate

masonry wall

1 x 2 furring

paneling

341

Embed tee in place with mortar. Space interior wall paneling and framing 2" away from tee, Illus. 341. A trim tee plate is fastened over this gap.

If you are going through a wood framed wall, Illus. 342, maintain the 2" clearance around tee. Install tee trim plate and flue cover. Cover exterior wall with metal flashing, Illus. 342.

Tees are available for both the 7 and 9" flue chimneys.

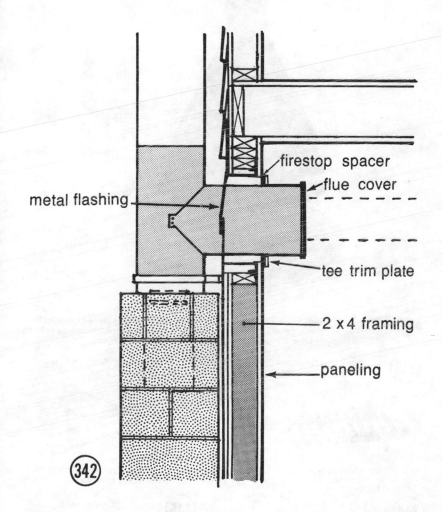

firestop spacer

flue cover

metal flashing

tee trim plate

2 x 4 framing

paneling

342

For those who prefer a round hearth, Illus. 326, one that can be filled with crushed stone, two different size rings are available. Both are shipped KD, Illus. 343. One measures 2" high and is 36" in diameter, the other is 3 x 42".

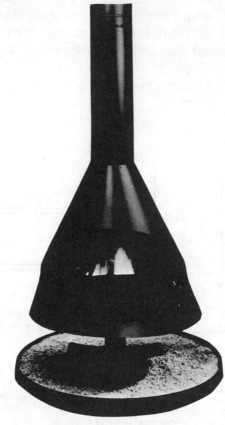

Hearth Ring

Handsome Flatte Black base illustrated with fireplaces. Available in four rugged rolled steel sections that bolt together; screw, nail or bolt to floor. Fill with any loose non-combustible material.

 Assembled Ring: —2" high x 36" diameter. —3" high x 42" diameter.

(343)

Grates

Heavy duty steel bar construction. Raises fire off hearth for better operation, holds fuel together for even burning.

(344)

Barbecue Grille

Chrome plated solid steel. Attaches firmly to fireplace hearth, easily removed for cleaning.

(345)

An attractive feature of the free standing fireplace, as well as those shown in Illus. 6, 10, is its use as a barbecue grille. Two accessories, a grate, Illus. 344, and a barbecue grille, Illus. 345, make picnicking at home a lot of fun.

FIREPLACES AVAILABLE

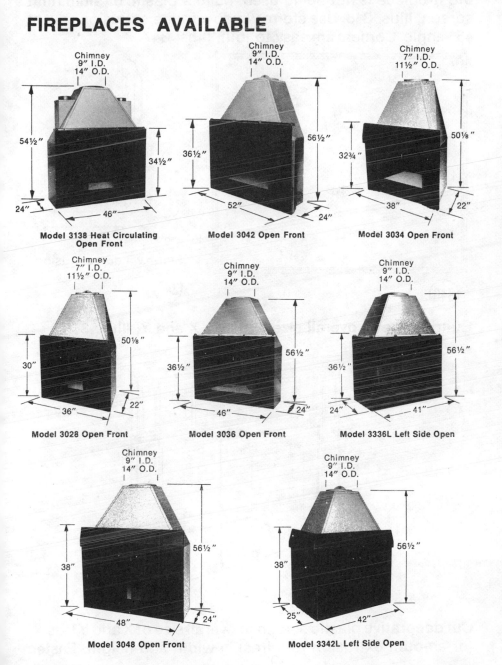

Chimney
9" I.D.
14" O.D.

54½"

34½"

24"

46"

Model 3138 Heat Circulating Open Front

Chimney
9" I.D.
14" O.D.

56½"

36½"

52"

24"

Model 3042 Open Front

Chimney
7" I.D.
11½" O.D.

50⅛"

32¾"

38"

22"

Model 3034 Open Front

Chimney
7" I.D.
11½" O.D.

50⅛"

30"

36"

22"

Model 3028 Open Front

Chimney
9" I.D.
14" O.D.

56½"

36½"

46"

24"

Model 3036 Open Front

Chimney
9" I.D.
14" O.D.

56½"

36½"

24"

41"

Model 3336L Left Side Open

Chimney
9" I.D.
14" O.D.

56½"

38"

48"

24"

Model 3048 Open Front

Chimney
9" I.D.
14" O.D.

56½"

38"

25"

42"

Model 3342L Left Side Open

237

HEAT SAVERS

Even the most efficient damper allows some room heat to escape up a flue. To offset this loss during those hours when the fireplace is not being used, build a plastic or aluminum screen, Illus. 346. Use storm window frame extrusions cut at 45° angle. Corners are easy to join, Illus. 347.

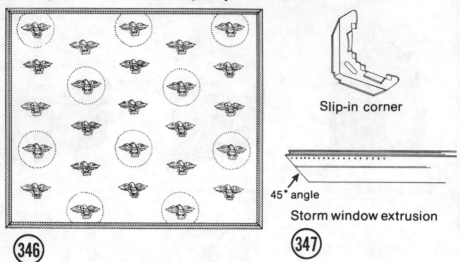

Slip-in corner

45° angle

Storm window extrusion

Build frame to overall size equal to X and Y, Illus. 348.

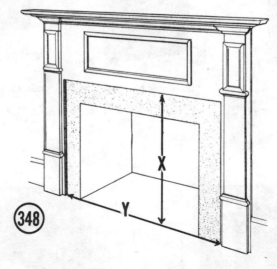

Cut decorative plastic screen to overall size of X and Y less 1'' (or amount extrusion requires) in width and height. Fasten screen to mantel around floor fireplaces with a pair of brass turn buttons, Illus. 349, available from marine supply stores.

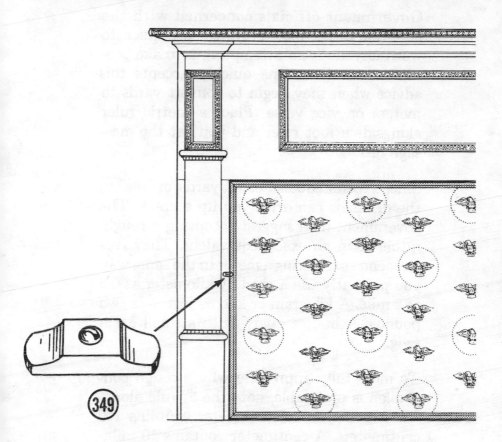

Drill two ¼" holes through frame of screen used to cover a raised fireplace. Hang same from two No. 8 screws inserted in expansion plugs, Illus. 309.

Apply 3/16 x ⅜" self adhesive plastic foam strip, Illus. 350, to inside face of frame.

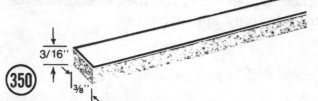

Never install screen over a hot fireplace.

HOW TO THINK METRIC

Government officials concerned with the adoption of the metric system are quick to warn anyone from attempting to make precise conversions. One quickly accepts this advice when they begin to convert yards to meters or vice versa. Place a metric ruler alongside a foot ruler and you get the message fast.

Since a meter equals 1.09361 yards, or 39⅜" +, the decimals can drive you up a creek. The government men suggest accepting a rough, rather than an exact equivalent. They recommend considering a meter in the same way you presently use a yard. A kilometer as 0.6 of a mile. A kilogram or kilo as just over two pounds. A liter, a quart, with a small extra swig.

To more fully appreciate why a rough conversion is preferable, note the 6" rule alongside the metric rule. A meter contains 100 centimeters. A centimeter contains 10 millimeters.

As an introduction to the metric system, we used a metric rule to measure standard U.S. building materials. Since a 1x2 measures anywhere from ¾ to ²⁵⁄₃₂ x 1½", which is typical of U.S. lumber sizes, the metric equivalents shown are only approximate.

Consider 1" equal to 2.54 centimeters;
10" = 25.4 cm.
To multiply 4¼" into centimeters: 4.25 × 2.54 = 10.795 or 10.8 cm.

EASY-TO-USE-METRIC SCALE

DECIMAL EQUIVALENTS

1/32		.03125
	1/16	.0625
3/32		.09375
	1/8	.125
5/32		.15625
	3/16	.1875
7/32		.21875
	1/4	.250
9/32		.28125
	5/16	.3125
11/32		.34375
	3/8	.375
13/32		.40625
	7/16	.4375
15/32		.46875
	1/2	.500
17/32		.53125
	9/16	.5625
19/32		.59375
	5/8	.625
21/32		.65625
	11/16	.6875
23/32		.71875
	3/4	.750
25/32		.78125
	13/16	.8125
27/32		.84375
	7/8	.875
29/32		.90625
	15/16	.9375
31/32		.96875

FRACTIONS — CENTIMETERS

1/16		0.16
	1/8	0.32
3/16		0.48
	1/4	0.64
5/16		0.79
	3/8	0.95
7/16		1.11
	1/2	1.27
9/16		1.43
	5/8	1.59
11/16		1.75
	3/4	1.91

(DECIMAL EQUIVALENTS continued)

13/16		2.06
	7/8	2.22
15/16		2.38

INCHES — CENTIMETERS

1		2.54
	1/8	2.9
	1/4	3.2
	3/8	3.5
	1/2	3.8
	5/8	4.1
	3/4	4.4
	7/8	4.8
2		5.1
	1/8	5.4
	1/4	5.7
	3/8	6.0
	1/2	6.4
	5/8	6.7
	3/4	7.0
	7/8	7.3
3		7.6
	1/8	7.9
	1/4	8.3
	3/8	8.6
	1/2	8.9
	5/8	9.2
	3/4	9.5
	7/8	9.8
4		10.2
	1/8	10.5
	1/4	10.8
	3/8	11.1
	1/2	11.4
	5/8	11.7
	3/4	12.1
	7/8	12.4
5		12.7
	1/8	13.0
	1/4	13.3
	3/8	13.7
	1/2	14.0
	5/8	14.3
	3/4	14.6
	7/8	14.9

EASY-TO-USE-METRIC SCALE

DECIMAL EQUIVALENTS

1/32		.03125
	1/16	.0625
3/32		.09375
	1/8	.125
5/32		.15625
	3/16	.1875
7/32		.21875
	1/4	.250
9/32		.28125
	5/16	.3125
11/32		.34375
	3/8	.375
13/32		.40625
	7/16	.4375
15/32		.46875
	1/2	.500
17/32		.53125
	9/16	.5625
19/32		.59375
	5/8	.625
21/32		.65625
	11/16	.6875
23/32		.71875
	3/4	.750
25/32		.78125
	13/16	.8125
27/32		.84375
	7/8	.875
29/32		.90625
	15/16	.9375
31/32		.96875

FRACTIONS — CENTIMETERS

1/16		0.16
	1/8	0.32
3/16		0.48
	1/4	0.64
5/16		0.79
	3/8	0.95
7/16		1.11
	1/2	1.27
9/16		1.43
	5/8	1.59
11/16		1.75
	3/4	1.91

13/16		2.06
	7/8	2.22
15/16		2.38

INCHES — CENTIMETERS

1		2.54
	1/8	2.9
	1/4	3.2
	3/8	3.5
	1/2	3.8
	5/8	4.1
	3/4	4.4
	7/8	4.8
2		5.1
	1/8	5.4
	1/4	5.7
	3/8	6.0
	1/2	6.4
	5/8	6.7
	3/4	7.0
	7/8	7.3
3		7.6
	1/8	7.9
	1/4	8.3
	3/8	8.6
	1/2	8.9
	5/8	9.2
	3/4	9.5
	7/8	9.8
4		10.2
	1/8	10.5
	1/4	10.8
	3/8	11.1
	1/2	11.4
	5/8	11.7
	3/4	12.1
	7/8	12.4
5		12.7
	1/8	13.0
	1/4	13.3
	3/8	13.7
	1/2	14.0
	5/8	14.3
	3/4	14.6
	7/8	14.9

3589 X